CERTIFIED
macromedia®
FLASH™ MX

Designer Study Guide

Christopher Hayes

macromedia®
FLASH™ MX
certified | DESIGNER

Certified Macromedia Flash MX Designer Study Guide
Christopher Hayes

Published by Macromedia Press, in association with Peachpit Press, a division of Pearson Education.

Macromedia Press
1249 Eighth Street
Berkeley, CA 94710
510/524-2178 800/283-9444
510/524-2221 (fax)

Find us on the World Wide Web at:
www.peachpit.com | www.macromedia.com
To report errors, please send a note to errata@peachpit.com

Macromedia Press Editor: Angela C. Kozlowski
Development Editor: Mark L. Kozlowski
Technical Editor: Matt Wobensmith
Production Coordinator: Connie Jeung-Mills
Copy Editor: Jacqueline Aaron
Index: Emily Glossbrenner
Proofreader: Haig MacGregor
Cover and Interior Design: Maureen Forys, Happenstance Type-O-Rama
Page Layout: Maureen Forys, Happenstance Type-O-Rama

ISBN 0-321-12695-5

9 8 7 6 5 4 3 2 1

Printed and bound in the United States of America

DEDICATION

To the Almighty, for His guidance and His many blessings. To Pop Pop, whose spirit will live in me forever. To Mom and Dad, for always being supportive in all that I do. And last but never least, to my lovely wife, for her love, support, and strength.

Acknowledgements

First and foremost, a thousand thanks to Angela Kozlowski and all at Macromedia Press for putting up with me. I've enjoyed working with you, and I thank you for giving me the opportunity to author this book. Thank you to the editors for your outstanding critiques and work. This book is ensured success because of your contributions.

Thank you to Niamh O'Byrne and Chrissy Rey for believing in me and asking if I would like to author this book. Both of you have provided tremendous support for me. I can't thank you enough.

Thank you to all my professors at Savannah College of Art and Design. To Dan Fantauzzi, please know that I am eternally grateful for all of your guidance and coaching while I was at SCAD. I will never forget when you came to visit me while I had that ruptured appendix in the hospital. May you rest in peace and know that you are never forgotten.

Thank you to all of my family at Xavier University. To John Scott, for always pushing me to the limit: You are one of the reasons that I am the man I am today. You nurtured me like your own son, and I thank you. To Dr. Charles Graves, who always managed to put a smile on my face no matter how tough the storm: You are the true reason I went into graphic and Web design. Your spirit will live and rejoice in me forever. May you rest in peace.

Thank you to all of my good friends. Mike McClellan of Designs in Motion, thank you for keeping me laughing, and for all of your support. You are a tremendous force in my life. To Victor Garcia, Simon Abrams, Ray Wade, Keith Barthelmeus, Shem Mathew, Wayne Scheiner, Ian Wilson, and Darryl White: Thank you for your continuous support and friendships.

Thank you to Jim and Chee, for your support and love. Without you two, I am nothing. To C.J., Maria, and Chrissy: Thanks for being the best brother and sisters a person could ever have. Thanks also to my lovely daughters, Victoria and Jordan, for keeping me young and focused.

And finally, a special thank you to the most dedicated, intelligent, beautiful, strong, selfless person that I have had the good fortune to be blessed with in my life—my soulmate Sabrina. Because of you, I am complete.

—Christopher Hayes
October 2002

CONTENTS AT A GLANCE

CONTENTS

ABOUT THE AUTHOR

Christopher Hayes is a Certified Macromedia Flash Designer and Subject Matter Expert. Since Chris helped write the Flash Designer Certification Exam, it seemed only right to have him write the study guide for it. He was also a contributing author of the book *Inside Flash*. Chris currently teaches the Fast Track to Macromedia Flash MX and Design Techniques with Macromedia Flash MX classes. He is the principal of Amalgamated Pixels, a custom design studio that specializes in multiple disciplines of graphic and Web design. He also spends time lecturing and speaking about Flash tips and tricks at Atlanta Macromedia User Group meetings. Chris currently resides in Atlanta with his wife, Sabrina, and their two children. Chris invites you to explore his Web site at www.amalgamatedpixels.com.

Introduction

With such widespread knowledge and use of the Macromedia Web tools, it makes sense to offer a certification exam to ensure that Web designers are confident and competent with these tools. This method will also help the many people who now style themselves as Web design experts. Macromedia Flash MX, one of the most widely used tools for creating Web sites and applications, is a good candidate for a certification test.

The development of the Flash certification exam naturally led to a companion study guide. Even Flash experts don't use every feature of the product or tackle every Web site design problem every day, and thus will want to spend some time reviewing before the exam. The content of this Study Guide will not only help you assure yourself that you're well versed in Flash and related technologies for Web site design, but will also prepare you for the certification process.

The approach of the Flash MX Study Guide is first to examine the overall Flash product and the tasks designers carry out with it, then to delve into the details. In this book you won't find an exhaustive study of every Flash feature or every client-side Web technology. You also won't find lots of tutorials and lengthy code examples. What you will find is a concise summary of Flash's salient features, arranged in order of increasing complexity, along with figures and examples that help demonstrate key points that a professional Flash designer should understand. You can learn how to use Flash from this book, but the idea is to reinforce and complement your knowledge with a summary of Flash's features and capabilities.

As you read through the book, you may be tempted to skip certain chapters. But while you may feel confident that you know all about a particular subject, you will find many tips and notes, as well as helpful information on limitations, of which you may not be aware. These could crop up in the certification test, so we recommend that you start from the beginning and take the time to study the pages in order. Of course, you can jump about all you want, but you should skim each chapter for important points (tips, cautions, and notes) before taking the test.

We hope you find this book useful, encapsulating as it does a wide variety of information in a succinct format. Good luck on the certification test!

What Is the Certified Flash Designer Exam?

The popularity of Macromedia's products continues to grow and, along with them, so has the demand for experienced designers. Once upon a time (in Internet time, that is), claiming to be a Flash designer was easy; the product was simple enough that with a minimal investment of time and energy, designers could realistically consider themselves experts.

This is not the case anymore. The Macromedia product line has grown in both breadth and complexity, and the levels of expertise and experience among designers are diverse. Claiming to be an expert isn't that easy, and recognizing legitimate expertise is even harder.

The Macromedia Certified Professional Program

This is where certification comes into play. Formal, official certification by Macromedia helps to mark a threshold that explicitly sets apart designers by their knowledge and experience, making it possible to identify the true experts.

The Certified Flash MX Designer certification is one in a series of certification tracks from Macromedia. This one is aimed at designers using Macromedia Flash MX. Other exams and certification programs being developed concentrate on other products and areas of expertise.

Reasons to Get Certified

There's really only one important reason for a Flash designer to become certified: Being able to call yourself a Macromedia Certified Flash MX Designer means you can command the respect and recognition that goes along with being one of the best at what you do.

Just as has happened with other products and technologies in this space, certification is likely to become a prerequisite for employers—an additional barometer by which to measure the potential of candidates and applicants.

Whether being certified helps you find a new or better job, helps persuade your boss that the pay raise you want is justified, helps you find new clients, or gets you listed on the Macromedia Web site so you can attract new prospects—whatever the reason—it will help you stand out from the crowd.

About the Exam

Becoming a Certified Flash MX Designer requires being tested on your knowledge of Flash MX and related technologies. As far as exams go, this one isn't easy—nor should it be. In fact, more than a third of all test takers fail their first exam. This is not a bad thing; on the contrary, it means that you really have to know your stuff to pass. You don't merely receive a paper certificate; the exam and subsequent certification have real value and real significance. "Very challenging but fair" is how many examinees describe the exam itself.

How You'll Take the Exam

The exam is a set of multiple-choice and true/false questions that you answer electronically. A computer application issues the test to you, and you'll know whether you passed immediately upon test completion.

In the test you're presented with each question and the possible answers. Some questions have a single correct answer, while others have two or more (you'll be told how many answers to provide). If a question stumps you, you can skip it and come back to it later.

After you have answered all the questions, you can review them to check your answers. After you're done, or after the 70-minute time limit is up, you get your results. You need to have at least 75 percent correct to pass and achieve certification. If you don't pass, you need to wait at least 30 days before you can try taking the test again. You may take the test no more than three times in a single year, starting from the date of your first test.

You will be required to pay the full exam fee each time you take the certification exam.

What You'll Be Tested On

Being a Flash MX expert requires knowing more than just how to use all the menu items. As such, the exam includes questions on related technologies. You will be tested on the following subjects:

- Project architecture, page and interface layout
- Effective visual design and scripting
- Effective motion design and ActionScripting
- Effective optimization and output design

Every question counts, and you can't assume that one particular topic is more or less significant than the others. You need to know it all, and you need to know it all well.

Preparing for the Exam

The most important preparation for the exam is using Flash MX itself. If you don't use it regularly or haven't done so for an extended period, you probably won't pass the exam.

Having said that, we can tell you that many experienced Flash MX designers still find the exam challenging. Usually, they say this is because they don't use some features and technologies, or because they learned the product but never paid attention to changing language and feature details (and thus are not using the product as effectively as they could be).

This is where this book fits in. This book is not a cheat sheet. It won't teach you Flash from scratch, nor will it give you a list of things to remember to pass the test. What it will do is help you systematically review every feature and technology in the product—everything you need to know to pass the test.

Where to Take the Exam

To offer the exams worldwide, in as many locations as possible, Macromedia has partnered with a company called VUE, which offers exams and certification programs for a wide range of companies and products, and has more than 2,500 regional testing facilities in more than 100 countries.

You can take the Macromedia Flash MX Designer exam at any VUE testing center. For a current list of locations, visit the Web site:

```
http://www.vue.com/macromedia/
```

How Much It Costs

The fee to take the exam in North America is $150 (U.S.). Pricing in other countries varies. The fee must be paid at the time you register for the exam. If you need to cancel, you must do so at least 24 hours before the exam, or the fee will not be refunded.

As a special gift to the readers of this book, and to encourage you to study appropriately for the test, Macromedia has sponsored a coupon that you can use for a discount off the exam fee. Refer to the coupon for details and usage information.

How to Use This Book

This book is designed to be used in two ways:

- To prepare for your exam, you should start at the beginning of the book and systematically work your way through it. The book flow, layout, and form-factor have all been designed to make reviewing content as pleasant an experience as possible. The content has been designed to be highly readable and digestible in small, bite-size chunks so that it will feel more like reading than studying.

- After you have reviewed all the content, reread the topics that you feel you need extra help brushing up on. Topics are all covered in highly focused and very manageable chapters so that you can easily drill down to the exact content you need. Extensive cross-referencing lets you read up on related topics as needed.

After the exam, you'll find that the style and design of this study guide make it an invaluable desktop reference tool as well.

Contents

The book is divided into four parts, each containing a set of highly focused chapters. Each chapter concludes with a summary and sample questions (the answers are in Appendix A).

Part I: Flash MX Basic Requirements: Project Architecture, Page and Interface Layout

This part covers the basics of using the Flash environment, page and interface layout, and Flash architecture. It includes chapters on the following topics:

- Page and interface layout

- Flash architecture

Part II: Effective Visual Design and Scripting

This part covers the tasks and technologies involved in building Flash documents, including type, color, and the tools used to create effective Flash documents. Chapters look at the following topics:

- Flash building blocks

- Using type

- Using color

- Tools

Part III: Effective Motion Design and ActionScripting

This part covers the features built into Flash to create animation and interactivity. It includes chapters on the following topics:

- Buttons

- Motion Design

- Introduction to ActionScript

- Events

- Variables

- Functions

- Objects

- Methods

Part IV: Effective Optimization and Output Design

This part covers sound and the testing, deployment, and maintenance of Flash documents. The section includes chapters on the following topics:

- Sound

- File size optimization

- Profiling

Conventions Used in This Book

The people at Peachpit Press have spent many years developing and publishing computer books designed for ease of use and containing the most up-to-date information available. With that experience, we've learned what features help you the most. Look for these features throughout the book to help enhance your learning experience and get the most out of Flash MX:

- Screen messages, code listings, and command samples appear in monospace type.

- URLs used to identify pages on the Web and values for Flash attributes also appear in monospace type.

- Terms that are defined in the text appear in *italics*. Italics are sometimes used for emphasis, too.

> **TIP**
>
> Tips give you advice on quick or overlooked procedures, including shortcuts.

> **NOTE**
>
> Notes present useful or interesting information that isn't necessarily essential to the current discussion, but that might augment your understanding with background material or advice relating to the topic.

> **CAUTION**
>
> Cautions warn you about potential problems that a procedure might cause, unexpected results, or mistakes that could prove costly.

→ Cross-references are designed to point you to other locations in this book that will provide supplemental or supporting information.

The Web Site

To further assist you in preparing for the exam, this book has an accompanying Web site. The site contains the following:

- Any updated exam information

- Links to other exam-related sites

- Any book corrections or errata

- A sample interactive test that you can use to help gauge your own exam readiness

The Web site can be found at `www.forta.com/books/0321126955`.

Where to Go From Here

Now you're ready to get started. If you think you're ready for the exam, start with the sample questions in the book or online to verify your skills. If you're not ready—or if the same questions indicate that you might not be as ready as you thought—make sure you pay attention to the topics that you need to review by reading the documentation and actually writing appropriate applications.

When you're ready, work through this book to review the content and prepare for the exam itself as described here.

And with that, we wish you good luck!

PART **1**

Flash MX Basic Requirements:

Project Architecture, Page and Interface Layout

CHAPTER 1

Page and Interface Layout

IN THIS CHAPTER

The Flash Interface

All Macromedia Flash MX document design is done within the authoring environment known as Macromedia Flash MX. The player and plug-in of Flash MX are known, respectively, as the Macromedia Flash Player 6 and the Macromedia Flash Player 6 plug-in.

The Flash MX authoring environment makes good use of screen real estate. If you've worked with Flash 5, you remember the numerous panels that could be opened at one time, taking up valuable screen space. Now Flash MX panels have two states: opened, as in the Color Swatches panel, and collapsed, as in the Color Mixer panel (see Figure 1.1).

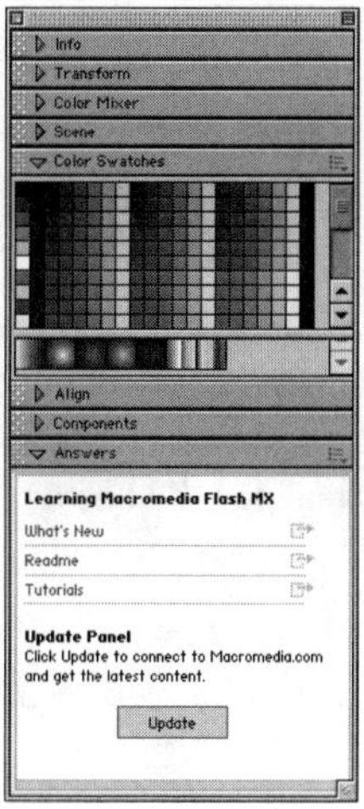

Figure 1.1
The difference between opened and collapsed panels is demonstrated here.

Also to save screen space, the Properties panel, also called the Properties Inspector, will populate with the appropriate attributes for the selected tool. Thus you can quickly edit the attributes of selected objects.

Note all the different elements that make up the Flash MX interface (see Figure 1.2). We will now introduce each major element, these are covered in greater detail later in the book.

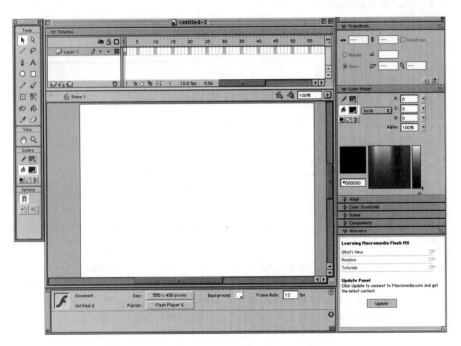

Figure 1.2   The Flash MX Interface is composed of various elements.

Introduction to the Timeline

A key component to the Flash MX interface, the Timeline is made up of layers (at the left side of the panel) and frames (at the right side of the panel) that let you organize and view the construction of a Flash MX movie (see Figure 1.3). Layers and frames are the two major components of the Timeline. You can expand or collapse either side of the Timeline by clicking and dragging the vertical division line between the two panes. The same holds true for the bottom division line between the Timeline panel and the stage.

By default, the Timeline is docked at the top of the Flash window, just above the stage. The Timeline can be moved to any position within the Flash window as a floating panel.

Figure 1.3

Layers and frames make up the Timeline.

→ All the functionality and attributes of the Timeline are covered in greater detail in Chapter 3, "Flash Building Blocks."

> **NOTE**
>
> As with all other panels, clicking the triangle next to the word Timeline at the top of the panel collapses the Timeline panel, freeing up valuable workspace.

Introduction to Layers

Layers are key to adding depth to your Flash MX movie. Think of layers as different tiers or levels of content that lie on top of each other. Layers are also used to organize a Flash MX movie. Note all the icons and features within the Layers pane (see Figure 1.4).

Figure 1.4

The Layers pane has many features and icons.

You can name, add, delete, and move layers. You can also hide and lock layers. By placing that content on its own layer, you can easily locate and manipulate that content. Also, by placing content on separate layers, you avoid any chance of the objects interacting with one another. When content is on its own layer, it becomes its own entity, allowing you to alter or manipulate it in any way you wish. You can now also manage layers with the new Insert Layer Folder option, which lets you place all layers with similar content or functionality into a titled folder.

Three icons can be found above the layers: the Show/Hide All Layers icon, the Lock/Unlock All Layers icon, and the Show All Layers As Outlines icon. To hide a layer, click the corresponding dot to the right of that layer's name, found below the Show/Hide All Layers icon. To see the contents of that layer again, simply click the same dot. To hide all the layers, click the Show/Hide All Layers icon. The same holds true for locking and unlocking layers and viewing layers as outlines.

Four more icons can be found below the layer pane: the Insert Layer icon, the Add Motion Guide icon, the Insert Layer Folder icon, and the Delete Layer icon. The guide layer lets you add guidance to any motion animations that you create. For example, you can make it look like a ball is bouncing onto the stage. When a layer is made into a guide layer, the contents of that layer that are seen in the authoring environment are not exported with the small Web format (SWF) file. Guide layers are used strictly as layout and design aids.

Also note the layer-stacking order: Whatever content is displayed in the top layer is what will be in the foreground of your Flash movie, and whatever content is displayed in the bottom layer will be in the background of your Flash movie. Therefore, background elements are usually placed in the bottom layer. To rearrange the layers, simply click and drag the layer into its new location within the layer stacking order.

→ For a detailed description of all the functionality and attributes of layers, see Chapter 3, "Flash Building Blocks."

> **NOTE**
>
> Oftentimes, Flash MX designers place all actions and labels on a single layer either at the top or the bottom of the layer stacking order. This makes it easy to manage and locate all frame actions and labels within a Flash MX movie.

Panels

Another major facet of the Flash MX authoring environment is panels. Panels allow you to manipulate virtually any element within your Flash movie. By default, Flash opens with the default panel set displayed. There are several panel set options that can be found under the Window option in the top menu bar. Depending on your monitor resolution and job description, you can select the panel set option that best works for you.

Each panel includes a ribbed title bar, a collapse triangle, and an options drop-down menu. The title bar, located at the top left of all panels, lets you click and drag a panel. You can dock panel within a panel set, and remove panels within a dock set to make them free-floating panels. Docking panels within a panel set lets you make better use of your screen real estate. Panels can be collapsed or opened by clicking the triangle at the top left next to the title bar. When collapsing a panel within a panel set, the entire panel set collapses, freeing up more screen real estate.

> **NOTE**
>
> If you rearrange your panel set and find yourself using that particular layout often, you can save that panel set layout by choosing Window > Save Panel Layout. Once you save it, that new layout will be available along with the original layout when you select Window > Panel Sets.

There is virtually a panel for every aspect of your Flash movie. Select any panel from the Window drop-down menu bar to display a particular panel. To close all panels, select Window > Close All Panels. See Table 1.1 for a list of the major panels and their individual functionalities.

> **TIP**
>
> A quick way to close all your panels is to press the Tab key on your keyboard. To get all the panels back, press the Tab key again.

Table 1.1 Major Flash MX Panels

PANEL	FUNCTIONALITY
Tools	All the tools needed to create objects, lines, and text can be found in the Tools panel. This panel is divided into four parts: Tools, View, Colors, and Options. Whenever a tool is selected within the Tools portion, the options for the selected tool change accordingly within the Options portion. You can zoom in and out of the stage area using the Zoom tool found in the View portion. You can also move the entire stage around when you select the Hand tool in the View portion. Utilizing the Colors portion of the Tools panel, you can change the fill and outline color of objects. Be sure to have the object selected that you would like changed, then click on the swatch drop-down menu and select a new color.
Properties	One of the biggest additions to Flash MX is the Properties panel, also known as the Properties Inspector. Similar to the Properties Inspector in Macromedia Dreamweaver MX, this panel gives you immediate information on any object or tool selected. The Properties panel groups features from other panels, depending on the object selected.
Align	The Align panel lets you line up objects either on the stage or to the stage. This panel is very useful when you need to align certain objects to direct center of the stage. To align objects, select the objects on the stage that need to be aligned to one another, and click the icon associated with what you wish to do. To align objects to the stage, select the objects to be aligned and be sure to click the To Stage icon. Next, click the icon associated with what you wish to do. You can also define distribution, size, and space of objects in the Align panel.
Info	In the Info panel you can quickly manipulate the width, height, and the x and y coordinates of any object within your Flash movie. Double-click within the text box of the attribute you wish to change, and type in the new information. The change will not take effect until you press the Tab or Return key.

Table 1.1 (CONTINUED)

PANEL	FUNCTIONALITY
Transform	The Transform panel lets you enlarge, reduce, rotate, or skew any object on the stage within your Flash MX movie. Check the Constrain option to limit height and width percentages.
Color Mixer	In the Color Mixer panel you can change the fill or outline color of selected objects. You can also dictate what type of fill you would like to create, and specify the alpha percentage of fills and outlines and the RGB values of a color. You can even type in a hexadecimal color here.
Color Swatches	The Color Swatches panel lets you quickly choose from a color palette of swatches. By default, Flash MX uses a Web-safe color palette, but you can load your own color palette here. You can also create and save gradients and colors in this panel.
Components	Another new feature to Flash MX is the convenience of the Components panel. Here you can find popular components for Flash MX user interfaces such as a check box, a list box, a combo box, and a Push key. Simply click and drag the component of your choice onto the stage and use the Properties Inspector to configure it.
Actions	The Actions panel is where all Macromedia Flash MX ActionScript is added to either an object or a frame within a Flash MX movie. The Actions panel is broken into three parts: the Actions library, the parameter pane, and the scripting window. Whenever an action is added, the parameter options change according to the action being added. When you're in Expert mode, the parameter pane disappears.

→ For more details on all the functionality and attributes of the Actions panel, see Chapter 9, "Introduction to ActionScript."

TIP

A quick way to close all your panels is to press the Tab key on your keyboard. To get all the panels back, press the Tab key again. To quickly erase everything on the stage, double-click the Eraser tool. If you double-click the eraser tool by accident, select Edit, Undo from the top drop-down menu bar.

The Flash Player

The Flash Player 6 is the device used to display the movies that you create in Flash MX. The Flash Player resides on your local hard drive, where it plays back movies in a stand-alone player or through a Web browser player.

> **NOTE**
>
> Many computers and Web browser applications ship with the Flash Player 6 included. You can download the Flash Player 6 and any upgrades from the Macromedia Web site.

Once within the Flash Player, a whole new menu system is available. There is the menu bar at the top of the screen and the right-click (Windows) or Control-click (Macintosh) pop-up menu. De-selecting the Display Menu option in the Publish Settings dialog box within the HTML tab disables this pop-up menu. You can also set Menu to false in the EMBED and PARAM HTML tags.

➜ For a detailed discussion covering all the functionality and attributes of the Flash Player 6, see Chapter 16, "File Size Optimization," and Chapter 17, "Profiling."

Printing Capabilities

You can print movies directly from the Flash Player 6 in two ways: either by using the Flash Player context menu and the Print command, or by using the ActionScript Print action. By using the Print action, you can print frames in any timeline of any movie clip or loaded movie level; you can also specify a certain print area.

> **NOTE**
>
> Flash Player versions earlier than 4 do not support direct printing from frames.

To designate a frame for printing, you must label the frame .#p. Frame labels are added through the Properties Inspector. To add a label, simply select the frame you wish to label. Once selected, type the label name within the Frame Label option within the Properties Inspector.

By default, the Flash MX movie's stage is what determines the print area. To specify a certain print area, create a shape on the stage the size of the newly desired print area. Make sure you do this in an empty frame. A good rule of thumb is to select the frame after the frame labeled #p. Label this new frame #b.

> **NOTE**
>
> You can add only one #b label per timeline, but you can add multiple #p labels to a timeline.

Summary

Flash MX is the authoring environment, and the Flash Player 6 is the device. The Timeline and panels are major elements within the Flash MX interface. The Timeline is made of two parts: layers and frames. Panels can be docked and collapsed to make better use of screen real estate.

Sample Questions

1. Which answer is true about the layer stacking order?

   A. The layer named Layer 1 will be in the foreground of the movie.

   B. The layer at the bottom will be in the foreground.

   C. The layer at the top will be in the foreground.

   D. The layer named Foreground will be in the foreground.

2. Which two answers of the following are true about panels?

   A. They have their own timelines.

   B. The Align panel aligns objects to the stage and to each other.

   C. The Align panel aligns objects to the stage only.

   D. The Properties panel is used to add actions.

   E. The Properties panel is used to add frame labels.

3. How are specific frames designated that will be printable from the Flash Player 6?

   A. Set formats in the Publish settings.

   B. Assign each frame the label #p.

   C. Assign each frame the label #b.

   D. Create the printable area shape on a frame labeled Print.

CHAPTER 2

Flash Architecture

IN THIS CHAPTER

Creating New Movies

The first step in creating an engaging and powerful Macromedia Flash MX experience is making a new Flash movie. A Flash movie document is denoted by an `.fla` file extension. When you launch Flash, by default a new, untitled document opens for you. You can also create a new Flash file by selecting File, New from the drop-down menu bar at the top. The Flash document is the file that contains all your movie's code and assets, such as pictures, audio, Macromedia ActionScript, and text.

Once you have a new Flash movie, you can alter its Document Properties by selecting Modify, Document, or Control-J (Windows) or Command-J (Macintosh) to open the Document Properties box (see Figure 2.1). Here you can change the movie's dimensions, background color, and frame rate.

> **TIP**
> You can also open the Document Properties box by double-clicking on the frames-per-second box found below the frames of the Timeline.

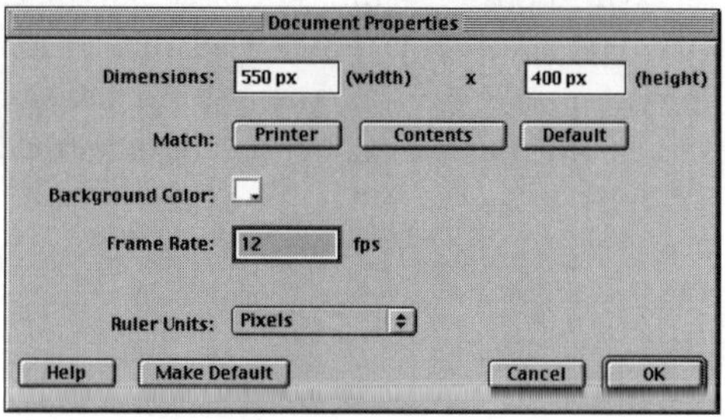

Figure 2.1

Here are the attributes of the Document Properties box.

Saving Movies

Once you've finished creating your movie, it's a good idea to save it right away and each time you make any changes to it. To save your movie, choose File, then Save, Save As, or Save As Template. Once you've saved your document, you can publish it to the Web by selecting File, Publish from the top menu bar. This creates a new file with the .swf (small Web format) file extension. This published SWF file is the one used or embedded in Web pages, or it can be used as a stand-alone application. Once a file has been published into an SWF file, all the assets become embedded and cannot be extracted from the file.

→ For detailed coverage of the functionality and attributes of the publishing process, see Chapter 16, "File Size Optimization."

Scenes

A Flash MX movie can be broken down into scenes, each of which is a separate section of the Timeline. However, scenes should be used only where appropriate. Since ActionScript cannot reference scenes within another part of the Timeline, it would better to use frame labels instead of scenes. In Flash movies with limited or no ActionScript, scenes work fine. The scene you are in is always noted above the stage area to the left. You can toggle through scenes quickly by clicking on the scene drop-down icon located above the stage area to the right. To find all the scenes within a Flash document, look in the Scene panel (see Figure 2.2).

Scenes work very similarly to layers from an organizational standpoint. You can duplicate, add, or delete a scene using the three icons at the bottom right of the Scene panel. You can also name and arrange your scenes here. To duplicate a scene in your Flash movie, select the desired scene and click the Duplicate Scene icon. To add a new scene to your Flash movie, click the Add Scene icon. To delete a scene from your Flash movie, click the Delete Scene icon. To rename a scene, double-click the scene name and type the new name. To go to a particular scene, double-click the scene icon next to the scene you're looking for.

Duplicating a scene can be very helpful for a number of reasons. Once you have placed all layers, actions, and content in one scene, you can duplicate it all, thus guaranteeing that all the contents and actions are in the same place and context. This way you don't have to spend all the time and effort you already put into creating that scene again. This saves you major design and development time. You can now simply rename this scene accordingly and change any content within the scene that would pertain to it alone.

Figure 2.2

The Scene panel houses all the scenes within a Flash document.

Scenes also have a stacking order. Whatever content is at the top of the scene stacking order is what will be played first in your Flash movie. For example, the scene titled "Preloader" in Figure 2.2 would play first, and the scene titled "Exit" would play last. To rearrange the scenes, simply click and drag the scene into its new location within the scene's stacking order.

Download Efficiency

As much as we like to fill our movies with eye-catching text effects and mind-blowing images and music, many people don't have the patience or the time to wait for big files to download over the Web. However, if you design your Flash MX movie with certain factors in mind, you can increase the download efficiency of your movie.

Sound Compression

One of the major factors that fattens your movie's file size is sound, so try to use it sparingly. If you do use sound, compress it as much as possible. Also, sync your sound to "stream," thereby forcing your Flash animations to keep pace with the audio. Moreover, a streamed sound never plays longer than the length of the frames in the timeline it occupies. If stereo isn't needed, use mono: It will cut your sound file size in half. Try to use the lowest sampling bit rate possible without sacrificing too much quality. Most of the time, end users view your movie on computers with inexpensive sound speakers, so big stereo sounds and high bit rates are just wasted.

Symbols

Another way to keep file sizes low is to reuse objects from the Library in Flash. If you have a forest scene, for example, convert one tree to a symbol and reuse that graphic symbol repeatedly to create your forest. Flash reads a forest of 300 trees the same way it reads a forest with 1 tree. In other words, Flash reads that tree only once, so the file size stays incredibly low.

Movie Loading

Another good way to improve download efficiency is to develop the movie in smaller pieces or SWFs as you create. ActionScript's loadMovie action will become your best friend. It lets you develop several smaller movies as opposed to one large movie. By using this approach, you empower your end users to load only what they want to see as opposed to waiting for an entire site to load. In order to load movies into your main movie, you have to specify a target location. To do this, you must designate the target's location area as a movie clip. You can also load a movie into a _level.

Finally, load important and crucial information—such as navigation and context—first, then load eye-candy animations and graphics last. That way users don't have to wait before gathering the important information.

Preloaders

A preloader is another name for a creative distraction. While a preloader plays, all your movie's contents load up so that once the movie has completed loading, it plays without interruption. The key thing to remember about preloaders is that they must remain simple and low in file size to allow for fast loading. By the time the preloader animation is finished, the rest of your movie will have successfully loaded.

Summary

Several of the main ways to increase the downloading efficiency of your Flash MX movie include sound compression, reuse of symbols, incremental movie loading, and preloaders.

Sample Questions

1. Which of the following increases download efficiency?

    A. Use the `attachMovie` script to allow multiple movies to play.

    B. Designate a target's location area as a graphic symbol.

    C. Load crucial information first and trivial animations last.

    D. A preloader should have intricate images and rich sound files.

2. Which two answers of the following are true about scenes?

    A. They can be duplicated.

    B. They can be created using the `loadScene` command.

    C. They can run independently of the main Timeline.

    D. They play back in the order listed in the Scene panel.

    E. They can be found in the Library.

3. When using symbols, which of the following is true?

    A. Flash reads a graphic symbol once no matter how many times it is used within the movie.

    B. Flash reads a graphic symbol every time it is used within the movie.

    C. Flash reads each part of the symbol several times.

    D. Flash only reads movie clips.

PART 2

Effective Visual Design and Scripting

Flash Building Blocks

Vector vs. Bitmap

Macromedia Flash MX is a vector-based application. Computers display graphics in either vector or bitmap format. Once you understand the difference between the two, you can begin to build more efficient Flash documents.

Vector graphics are drawn mathematically. They are based on the points of an object. The color, shape, size, and position of the object can change without losing any quality of its appearance. Vector graphics are also resolution independent, meaning they can be displayed on monitors with different screen resolutions and not forfeit a bit of quality (see Figure 3.1).

Bitmap graphics are images that use an amalgamation of pixels. When you modify a bitmap graphic, you change pixels as opposed to lines and curves. Bitmap graphics are resolution dependent because the pixels are fixed to a grid of a specific size (see Figure 3.1).

Figure 3.1

A close-up reveals the difference between vector and bitmap graphics.

Vector   Bitmap

Symbols

To perform a number of tasks, Macromedia Flash depends on the usage and instance of symbols. Symbols are reusable elements that you use throughout your Flash documents. Once you create a symbol, which can be anything from text to a sound file, it is automatically tracked in the Library. Each symbol has its own timeline and layers associated with it. There are three types of symbol behaviors: graphics, movie clips, and buttons.

Types of Symbol Behaviors

A graphic symbol is usually a static image that is incorporated into the main Timeline. Interactive controls and sounds don't work within a graphic symbol's animation sequence.

A movie clip symbol is usually an animation sequence that has its own timeline and works independently of the main Timeline. Interactive controls and sounds do work within a movie clip symbol's animation sequence. A movie clip can contain another movie clip, graphic, or button. You can even place an instance of a movie clip within a button for an animated sequence within your button. ActionScript can also speak to or affect instances of movie clips.

> **NOTE**
> The animation and scripts created within a movie clip cannot be seen within the Flash MX authoring environment. To see the effects of your movie clips, you have to view them in the Flash Player.

A button symbol is used to—you guessed it—create buttons. These buttons allow for interactivity within your Flash document. Its timeline consists of four states: up, over, down, and hit.

→ All the functionality and attributes of buttons are covered in greater detail in Chapter 7, "Buttons."

Creating and Editing Symbols

You can create symbols in Flash either by converting an existing object on the stage to a symbol or by creating an empty symbol and designing the symbol within its symbol-editing mode.

To convert an existing element on the stage into a symbol, select the object on the stage. Then either select Insert, Convert to Symbol from the top menu bar, or right-click (Windows) or Control-click (Macintosh) and toggle down to Convert to Symbol from the pop-up menu. Once you do that, the Convert to Symbol dialog box appears. Within this dialog box you can specify a name, a behavior, and the registration point of the symbol. Once you click OK, the symbol is automatically loaded into your Library. All editing to this symbol must thereafter be done in symbol-editing mode. Flash MX also allows you to simply drag content to the Library window to create a symbol.

To create a new symbol, select Insert, New Symbol from the top menu bar. You will notice that the Create New Symbol dialog box appears. Within this dialog box, you can specify a name, a behavior, and the registration point of the symbol. Once you click OK, the symbol is automatically loaded into your Library.

TIP

Simply double-click a symbol to bring it into symbol-editing mode. To get back to your movie, select the original scene from the breadcrumb trail located to the top right of the stage.

The Library

All the symbols and assets of a Flash document are found within its own Library. As discussed earlier, graphics, buttons, and movie clips are automatically housed here whenever you create a new symbol or convert objects to symbols.

The Library window is one of the major components of the Flash interface (see Figure 3.2). Whenever a new Flash document is created, the Library is empty. You can open the Library window by selecting Window, Library from the top menu bar. If you want to use some assets or symbols from another Flash movie, simply select File, Open As Library from the top menu bar. Then you just click and drag the symbols you want to use into either the current movie's stage or its Library.

The Library window has a list of symbols and assets currently being used in your movie. The Preview pane located at the top shows which symbol is selected. There are also four icons located along the bottom of the window, which, respectively, let you create a new symbol, create a new folder, change the properties, and delete items within the Library. Folders are used to manage and organize the elements

Figure 3.2

The Library is where all symbols are stored.

within the Library. Each element has a unique icon displayed next to it. The Library window lets you expand and collapse the window. If you click the expand icon, you will see that you can view the symbol's property type or kind, and use count, linkage, and modification-date attributes of each asset within the Library. The drop-down menu offers many other options, which are listed in Table 3.1.

Table 3.1 The Library's Menu Options

MENU OPTION	MEANING
New Symbol	Creates a new symbol. This new symbol is then placed immediately into the Library.
New Folder	Creates a new folder within the Library.
New Font	Opens the Font Symbol Properties dialog box. This allows the font symbol to be used in a shared Library.
New Video	Creates a new video in the Library into which a video is imported.
Rename	Allows you to rename a selected symbol.
Move to New Folder	Opens the New Folder dialog box.
Duplicate	Duplicates the selected symbol.
Delete	Deletes the selected symbol.
Edit	Opens Symbol Editing Mode.
Edit With	Launches an external application that lets you edit the selected symbol based on its symbol type.
Properties	Opens the Symbol Properties dialog box.
Linkage	Opens the Linkage Properties dialog box.
Component Definition	Opens the Component Definition dialog box.
Select Unused Items	Searches and finds all unused Library items.
Update	Updates the Library of all imported items that have been edited or modified after import.
Play (Stop)	Plays (or stops playing) the selected symbol in the Preview pane.
Expand Folder	Opens the selected folder.
Collapse Folder	Closes the selected folder.
Expand All Folders	Opens all folders.
Collapse All Folders	Closes all folders.
Shared Library Properties	Opens the Shared Properties dialog box for use with shared libraries.
Keep Use Counts Updated	Provides updates of the Use Counts field.

Table 3.1   (CONTINUED)

MENU OPTION	MEANING
Update Use Counts Now	Updates the Use Counts field.
Help	Opens Web browser for online help with the Library.
Maximize Panel	Opens the Library window to full view.
Close Panel	Closes the Library.

The Timeline

As mentioned earlier, the Timeline is made up of two major components: frames (at the right side of the panel) and layers (the left side of the panel.) These two key attributes of the Timeline let you organize and view the construction of a Flash movie. The numbers above the Timeline in multiples of five indicate frames—one of the major building blocks of a Flash movie.

Frames

A frame in Flash is the equivalent to a cell in film. Frames are what give a Flash movie its duration. The more frames you add, the longer your Flash movie will be. You can add, delete, move, cut, copy, clear, and/or paste frames anytime.

There are several ways to insert a frame within the Timeline. To insert a new frame, first select within the Timeline where you would like to place the new frame. Then select Insert, Frame from the top menu bar. You can also right-click (Windows) or Control-click (Macintosh) to display the pop-up menu and toggle down to choose the Insert Frame option.

> **NOTE**
> Notice that within the drop-down menus from the top menu bar, keyboard shortcuts are displayed just to the right of several menu options. To insert a frame, you can also press the F5 key on your keyboard.

Performing other functions to a frame is done in a similar way. To delete a frame, select Insert, Remove Frames from the top menu bar, or choose the Remove Frames option from the pop-up menu. To cut, copy, clear, and/or paste a frame, select the appropriate option from Edit in the top menu bar or select the appropriate option from the pop-up menu.

You can also move a frame to a new location within the Timeline by using the mouse to select and drag a frame to a new location. There are two types of frames: regular frames and keyframes.

Keyframes

Keyframes are used whenever there is a point of change in a Flash movie. Keyframes are usually used within frame-by-frame, motion-tween, and shape-tween animation. To create a keyframe, select the frame where you wish to insert. Then, either select Insert, Keyframe or right-click (Windows)/Control-click (Macintosh) and toggle down to Insert Keyframe in the pop-up menu. Whenever you do this, the contents from the previous keyframe are automatically brought over into this new keyframe. Choose Blank Keyframe if you simply want to insert an empty keyframe.

Frame Labels

Labels become useful to identify particular frames, including keyframes, in a Flash document. They give you an alternative to scenes and frame numbers to talk to your Flash document through ActionScript. To add a label to a frame, select the frame, then select the text box under Frame within the Properties Inspector, and type in the label name of your choice.

Try to avoid long frame names because frame labels are exported with your movie. If you need to provide a good bit of information for a particular frame, use a comment, since it will not be exported with the movie data. To create a comment, precede the text with two forward slashes (//).

Frame Rates

Frame rates, the current frame number, and elapsed time are displayed at the bottom of the Timeline. You can set the frame rate of a Flash document anywhere from 0.01 to 120 frames per second (fps). By default, Flash sets a frame rate of 12 fps. If you want to increase or decrease the frame rate of a particular section, it's best to add or delete frames in between the keyframes of the animation. To increase or decrease the frame rate of an entire document, select Modify, Document from the top menu bar and type in the new frame rate.

Multiple Timelines

By default, a single timeline is attached to your Flash document. Using movie clips, you can now have multiple timelines, nesting them within other movie timelines. This is possible because each movie has its own timeline. Whenever you have a timeline that involves other movie clips, those timelines are invoked by the master Timeline, and the multiple timelines communicate and interact with one another.

Layers

The other major component of the Timeline is layers. Just as frames add duration or length to a Flash movie, layers add dimension or depth to a Flash movie. Think of layers as different tiers of content that lay on top of each other.

Flash MX introduces layer folders. Working very similarly to the folders in the Library, layer folders can be used to organize and group layers. Layer folders also expand and collapse so you can see which layers are contained within the layer folder. Layer folders can have more folders within them for precise layer-filing structures. Locking a layer folder locks all the layers within that folder.

Creating, Viewing, and Editing Layers or Layer Folders

Layers or layer folders can be added in many different ways. The most common way is to click the Insert Layer icon found below the layers within the Layers pane. You can also either right-click (Windows) or Control-click (Macintosh) on a layer and toggle down to the Insert Layer option in the pop-up menu; or select Insert, Layer from the top menu bar. Whenever a layer or layer folder is added, it automatically becomes the active layer.

Layers or folders can be made hidden or visible by clicking the dot under the Show/Hide All Layers icon. Although a layer or folder may be hidden in the Flash authoring environment, it is exported in the SWF file. All layer contents except the Guide Layer content are exported to the small Web format (SWF) file.

Whenever a layer is active and editable, a pencil icon appears next to the layer name in the Layer pane. Although you can select more than one layer at a time, only one layer can be active at any given time. To delete a layer, select the layer and either click the Delete Layer icon, drag the layer to the Delete Layer icon, or choose Delete in the pop-up menu.

Guide Layers

Guide layers help you align objects when creating your Flash document. These layers don't appear in your final SWF file; therefore, they don't add to your final SWF file size. Guide layers come in handy for controlled motion guides that allow an animation to take place along a specified path. A motion path is created within the guide layer to provide a way to create movement along this path from a start point to an end point. The guide layer has an icon of a dotted line in an arched formation next to it.

A single guide layer can affect or guide multiple layers. The layers you want affected must appear below the guide layer. The visual indicator that they are indeed being affected by the guide layer is a right indent in the layers icon and name (see Figure 3.3).

Figure 3.3

The guide layer can affect multiple layers.

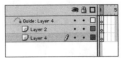

Any layer can become a guide layer. To create a guide layer, select the layer and either click the Add Motion Guide icon or choose Add Motion Guide option in the pop-up menu.

Mask Layers

As previously stated, objects that are on higher layers within the layer stacking order appear in front of objects in lower layers. In a similar fashion, a mask layer appears on top of the layer it is affecting within the layer stacking order. A mask layer is a layer that lets you specify which areas of the layer below it will be visible in your final presentation. For example, if you wanted to create the illusion of rain falling outside a window, and you want the rain to show only within that window's frame or designated area, you would use a mask.

The mask layer has a rectangle icon with a transparent oval within it. As with the guide layer, the visual indicator that a layer is masked is an indentation to the right. The mask layer can mask multiple layers for more complex effects. You can also click and drag a layer in between the mask layer and the layer it is masking to have it included within the masked area (see Figure 3.4).

Figure 3.4

The mask layer can also affect a number of layers.

The objects on the mask layer will not be visible in the final presentation. You can see only the objects on the mask layer within your authoring environment.

> **NOTE**
> The mask layer and the layers it masks are locked in the layers' windowpane. As long as these layers are locked, you will see your mask effect within the authoring environment. Once you unlock one of them, you will not see the mask effect within the authoring environment.

To create a mask layer, right-click (Windows) or Control-click (Macintosh) the layer that you want to designate your mask layer. Choose Mask from the pop-up menu.

Summary

Flash MX is a vector-based application. Its major building blocks include symbols, the Timeline, frames, and layers. The Library houses all symbols created within a document, and the Timeline houses all frames and layers. There are three behavior types of symbols: movie clips, graphics, and buttons. The guide layer and mask layer are two forms of specialized layers.

Sample Questions

1. Which two answers of the following are true about vector-based graphics?

   A. Vector-based graphics are resolution dependent.

   B. Vector-based graphics are drawn mathematically.

   C. Vector-based graphics appear pixelated when enlarged.

   D. Vector-based graphics do not appear pixelated when enlarged.

2. Which two of the following items does the Timeline house?

   A. Layers.

   B. Keyframes.

   C. Symbols.

   D. Movie clips.

   E. None of the above.

3. Which of the following is false about the Timeline?

   A. The Timeline houses frames, keyframes, and layers.

   B. The Timeline houses frames and mask layers.

   C. The Timeline houses frames, symbols, and layers.

   D. The Timeline houses layers.

CHAPTER 4

Using Type

Creating Text

You can include several kinds of text in your Macromedia Flash MX document. You can create static text for buttons or menu items, and you can create static text blocks where you just need the text to be within this specified area. You can also create input text boxes—for data entry forms, for example—and dynamic text boxes that import text from an external source such as stock quotes or daily news.

> **NOTE**
> Text can be displayed horizontally with left-to-right flow, or vertically (for static text only) with left-to-right or right-to-left flow.

You can alter the point size, font, style, color, spacing, and alignment of your text. You can transform text just as you would with an object, by rotating, skewing, or scaling it. Text can also be broken apart and reshaped. You can hyperlink text to URLs. You can also embed fonts in your Flash document. Doing this ensures that end users will see exactly what you intended them to see, and you're no longer limited to the fonts someone may or may not have loaded on their computer. However, this technique adds to the final file size.

You can create a symbol from a font. This lets you export the font as part of a shared library and allows for the use of that font in other Flash MX documents.

You cannot spell-check text in Flash. In order to spell-check text, you need to copy and paste it into an external text-editor application.

To create text, select the text tool from the toolbar. To type static text, click on the stage and begin typing. To create a static text box, click and then drag to the desired text-field length and width. The same holds true when creating a dynamic text box or an input text box. Once you've used the text tool to create your text on the stage, use the Properties panel (also called the Properties Inspector) to define what type of text field you would like. Within the Properties panel, you can determine all the other attributes of your text.

Although you can apply any attribute to alter static text, you cannot use certain attributes on dynamic text fields. Such attributes include kerning, character spacing, hyperlinking, rotation, and direction of text. With input fields, you have other options such as word wrap and text borders. You can apply instance names to dynamic text and input text fields, but not to static text.

In order to create scrollable text, you must use the dynamic text option and then give it an instance name. Once you do this, you can then attach the scroll bar component to this dynamic text field.

Flash displays a specific handle on the corner of the text field to identify what type of text field you are creating. For a list of text fields and their corresponding handles, see Table 4.1.

Type Attributes

You can determine the following attributes of text in the Properties panel (see Figure 4.1).

Figure 4.1

Use the Properties panel to alter text attributes.

Font attributes include the following:

- Font family
- Point size
- Style (bold or italic)
- Color
- Character spacing
- Character position
- Kerning
- Text type
- Text direction

- Device fonts

- Borders

- HTML

- Selectability

- URL link

- x and y coordinates

- Width and height

Paragraph attributes include the following:

- Alignment

- Indents

- Margins

- Line spacing

- Format

You can set the font and paragraph attributes of text. Kerning is the spacing between letters or characters. Many fonts have built-in kerning information. For example, the space between an F and an I may be different from the space between an F and a T. In order to use the font's built-in kerning information, check the Auto Kern option in the Properties panel.

In order to manipulate any of these attributes, you must have the text selected first.

Embedded Fonts vs. Device Fonts

When using a font installed on your computer, Flash embeds the font information into the small Web format (SWF) file. This ensures that the font is displayed within the Flash Player 6 as you designed it in your authoring environment.

You also have the option of using special fonts called "device fonts" as a substitute for embedded fonts. There are three device fonts in Flash MX: _sans (similar to Arial or Helvetica), _serif (similar to Times Roman), and _typewriter (similar to Courier). Device fonts—which can be used for both static and dynamic text—are not embedded into your final Flash presentation. Instead, the fonts that most closely resemble the device fonts used in your movie are found on the end user's computer and used.

> **CAUTION**
> While using device fonts gives you a smaller file size, there is no guarantee how the text within the presentation will display on the end user's computer screen.

Dynamically Updating Text

You can update dynamic text fields through an external text file. This is extremely helpful for updating daily news and anything that may need to change on a daily basis. With dynamic text fields in place, you never have to open your Flash document again to update text. Your dynamic text field is scripted to read from an external text file. Your text file can be created using a text editor application such as Notepad (PC) or SimpleText (Macintosh).

To create a dynamic text field, select your text tool. Click and drag a text field onto your stage. Once the text field is drawn, make sure it is selected, then choose the Dynamic option from the Text Type drop-down menu option in the Properties panel. Like a movie clip, dynamic text can have an instance name. By naming this dynamic text field with an instance name, you can talk to it through Action-Script. You then need to place ActionScript code that will load data or variables (loadVariables) into this dynamic text field from your external text file.

→ For more details about this and other simple ActionScript techniques, see Chapter 9, "Introduction to ActionScript."

Creating Font Symbols

You create a font symbol from the Library panel's option menu. Once this is done, you can use this font as a shared library item. Assign the font symbol an identifier string and a URL where the movie containing the font symbol will be located. This lets you link to this font without embedding it within your movie, thus shaving a few pounds off your final file size.

Linking Text to URLs

To link text to a URL, select the text to be linked. With the text selected, type the URL link to which you want the end user directed within the URL Link of the Properties panel. To create a link to an email address, simply use the mailto: prefix in front of your URL link, which in this case would be the specified email address. Thus it would read mailto:yourname@yourcompany.com within the URL Link.

Summary

There are three types of text format: static, input, and dynamic. There are multiple attributes that can be edited for text through the Properties panel. Embedded fonts are embedded in your Flash document, guarantee that what you've designed will be what any end user sees, and add to your final file size. Device fonts are not embedded in your Flash document, do not guarantee what the end user sees, and do not add to your final file size.

Sample Questions

1. Which of the following is true about device fonts?

   A. Device fonts add to your final file size.

   B. Device fonts are embedded within your final file.

   C. Device fonts do not guarantee the final viewed result is what you designed.

   D. Device fonts can be found only on your computer.

2. Which two of the following items are types of text formats?

   A. Static.

   B. Embedded.

   C. Rotating.

   D. Device.

   E. Input.

3. Which of the following is true about dynamic text fields?

   A. They can be used for static text.

   B. They can be used for static block text.

   C. They can be altered by every text attribute.

   D. They are used for scrollable text.

CHAPTER **5**

Using Color

One of the most important aspects of good design is the appropriate use of color. Color plays a powerful role in setting the mood of a presentation. A company's brand is defined mostly by color. Color can indicate different sections throughout a presentation, and add emphasis to specific areas.

Manipulating color within Macromedia Flash MX is a snap. A precise color palette to select from helps keep your presentation consistent and unified. Flash provides four main tools that help you work with color:

- The Color Mixer panel lets you mix new colors, as well as change the stroke and fill colors of an object. You can also specify the fill attributes here.

- The Color Swatches panel allows you to track colors used in a Flash document.

- The Eyedropper tool lets you sample color from anywhere within your Flash authoring environment, the Color Mixer, or from color swatches.

- The Properties panel lets you adjust the fill and stroke attributes.

> **NOTE**
> Another place you can adjust an object's fill and stroke color is the Colors section of the toolbar.

In addition to changing the color attributes of an object, you can change the color of symbols and symbol instances. Let's say you have a green circle graphic symbol that appears in a document. It's used quite a bit, and you need to change its color attribute to red throughout the entire presentation. The quickest way to do this is to open the circle in symbol editing mode. Once in symbol editing mode, the fill attribute can be swiftly changed to red. Since you made this change within the graphic symbol, the circle is now red everywhere it appears within your Flash document.

> **NOTE**
>
> There are three ways to get to symbol editing mode:
>
> ■ You can create a new symbol, which automatically brings you to symbol editing mode.
>
> ■ You can double-click on that particular symbol on the stage.
>
> ■ You can double-click the symbol within the Library.

The beauty of symbols is that Flash renders a symbol only once. It can be used over and over again without adding additional file size to your final movie. Utilizing the same example, whether you have one circle graphic symbol or 200 graphic symbols on the stage, your final movie will be the same size because Flash only needs to render that graphic symbol once.

Using the same example, let's say you need to change only an instance of the green circle graphic symbol. Using the Properties panel, you can change its color attributes by altering its tint, brightness, alpha, or all three through the Advanced option. Using the Color drop-down menu within the Properties Inspector can change all of these options.

The Color Mixer

As previously mentioned, one place to change color attributes is the Color Mixer (see Figure 5.1). The Color Mixer lets you determine a specific stroke or fill color for an object. You can also dictate whether a particular fill color is a solid, linear gradient, radial gradient, or bitmap fill.

Figure 5.1

The Color Mixer can be used to adjust color attributes.

Changing Fill Color

The Color Mixer makes it easy for you to change an object's fill color or its fill color attributes. You can change a color by adjusting the RGB values of a selected color. You can also adjust color by typing in hexadecimal code. You can change an object's fill color by selecting a new swatch from the swatch drop-down menu. You can also adjust the transparency of a fill by using the Alpha property text field.

To change the fill attribute, select the Linear or Radial Gradient option from the fill drop-down menu. Notice that you get new options in the Color Mixer to help you adjust or modify the gradient you've just created (see Figure 5.2). To add gradient handles, simply click anywhere beneath the gradient bar. To remove gradient handles, click and drag down.

Figure 5.2

The Color Mixer provides new options for a gradient.

If you have any bitmaps in your document, you can use the Bitmap fill option to fill an object with that particular bitmap.

> **TIP**
>
> You can use the Paint Bucket tool to manipulate your gradients. When using a radial gradient, click the paint bucket where you want your light source to come from on the object. When using a linear gradient, click and drag the paint bucket tool along the object to control the direction and display of the gradient.

Changing Stroke Color

In much the same way the Color Mixer lets you change the fill color, it also makes it easy to change an object's stroke color or stroke color attributes. You can change a color by adjusting the RGB values of a selected color. You can also adjust color by typing in hexadecimal code. Or you can change an object's stroke color by selecting a new swatch from the swatch drop-down menu. Finally, you can adjust a stroke's transparency by using the Alpha property text field.

The Color Swatches Panel

The Color Swatches panel houses all the color and swatches used in a Flash document (see Figure 5.3). The Color Swatches panel lets you quickly see what color palette is being used in a document.

Figure 5.3

The Color Swatches panel lets you track colors used in a document.

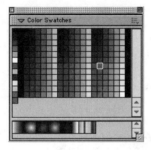

Creating Custom Color Swatches

Whenever you create a custom color in the Color Mixer, you have the option to add it by using the Color Mixer's options pop-up menu. When you choose Add Swatch here, it is added as a swatch in the bottom portion or pane of the Color Swatches panel. You can then use this added swatch in your Flash document whenever you want. This way, there is no need to try and re-create a particular gradient you made previously, and you're guaranteed consistency throughout your presentation.

Swatch File Extensions

RGB swatch palettes or files can be imported and exported between Flash documents by using the options in the Color Swatches panel. These files are known as Flash Color Set or .clr files. You can also import and export RGB color palettes using Color Table files or .act files. These files can be used with Macromedia Fireworks and Adobe Photoshop.

To import a color palette to a document, choose either Add Colors or Replace Colors from the Color Swatches panel's options pop-up menu. Find the file, select it, and click OK.

To export a color palette, choose Save Colors from the Color Swatches panel's options pop-up menu. In the pop-up dialog box, type the specific name you wish to call your color palette. Choose Flash Color Set or Color Table for the Save As Type (Windows) or Format (Macintosh). Click Save.

Web-Safe Colors

Since all Web browsers and monitors are different, some find it reassuring to use Web-safe colors. Although this palette can be limiting, it assures the designer that the end user will see the exact color chosen, ultimately giving the designer more control over the design. Flash gives you the option to load the Web-safe 216-color palette. Within the Color Swatches panel's options, simply choose Web-216.

Summary

There are several ways to change the color attributes of an object. You can also change the color attributes of symbols. The Color Mixer and the Color Swatches panels play key roles in letting you create and change color. Palettes can be imported into and exported from a Flash document.

Sample Questions

1. Which of the following is considered a swatch file extension?

   A. .txt

   B. .psd

   C. .png

   D. .clr

   E. .ctr

2. Which of the following does the Color Swatches panel let you do?

   A. Create new colors

   B. Export a color palette

   C. Alter an object's color attributes

   D. Change an object's stroke color

3. Which two of the following does the Color Mixer let you do?

   A. Load palettes

   B. Save palettes

   C. Add swatches

   D. Save both palettes and swatches

   E. Create potential swatches

CHAPTER 6

Tools

Macromedia Flash MX provides multiple tools for creating and modifying objects in a Flash document. Most of the tools in the toolbar are used for drawing and painting (see Figure 6.1). Whenever you choose a specific drawing or painting tool, the Properties Inspector changes to display the appropriate attributes for that particular tool.

The stroke or fill color that is selected will be the stroke and fill attributes of any object drawn with the painting or drawing tools. These attributes can be changed before or after creating an object. If you change these attributes after you draw, be sure you select the object first, then apply your modifications.

→ All of the functionality and attributes of color are covered in greater detail in Chapter 5, "Using Color."

Figure 6.1

The toolbar contains mostly drawing and painting tools.

Transform Capabilities

There are a variety of ways to transform objects within a Flash document:

- The Transform tool

- The Transform panel

- Right-click (Windows) or Control-click (Macintosh) on the object to be altered

- The Properties panel

- Choose Modify, Transform from the top menu bar

The Transform tool lets you free-transform any text or object in a Flash document. Free-transforming includes rotating, scaling, skewing, and distorting. The Transform tool can't distort symbols, videos, or bitmaps.

> **TIP**
>
> To constrain the proportions of the object being altered, Shift-click and drag the object until you achieve the desired size.

The Transform panel can also be used to alter an object (see Figure 6.2). Here you can specify a transform percentage, or type in a specific degree of rotation or skew. You can also limit the width and height by clicking the Constrain option in the panel.

Figure 6.2

The Transform panel can also be used to alter an object.

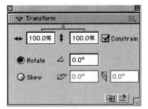

Drawing Tools

As mentioned earlier, a majority of the tools in the toolbar are drawing tools. You use these tools to create objects within your Flash file, whether it be a line or a shape. Table 6.1 outlines the different drawing tools and their utilization.

Table 6.1 Tools for Drawing

TOOL	UTILIZATION
Line	To create straight lines
Pencil	To create free-form, straight, and curved lines
Pen	To create lines using anchor points
Oval	To create circle and oval objects
Rectangle	To create square and rectangle objects

Line Tool

You use the Line tool whenever you need to create a straight line. The line is drawn from click to release. By holding the Shift key while drawing, you get straight lines in increments of 45 degrees. To draw connected lines, simply click and drag again immediately after releasing the last line segment. The current stroke attributes are displayed when you draw a line segment. Fill attributes don't affect line-tool drawings.

Pencil Tool

The Pencil tool mimics a pencil by letting you draw free-form shapes and segments. You create lines with the Pencil tool the same way you would create a line with the Line tool: click, drag, release. The current stroke attributes will be displayed when you draw the line segment.

The Pencil tool has three modifiers associated with it: Straighten, Smooth, and Ink. These modifiers can be located within a drop-down menu within the Options portion of the toolbar. The straighten modifier straightens line segments created with the Pencil tool. The smooth modifier provides a smoother line result without the harsh angles and edges that the straighten modifier produces. The ink modifier doesn't smooth or straighten; rather, it draws the segment as close to form as you created it.

Pen Tool

Unlike the Pencil tool, the Pen tool is used to draw precise lines and curves, as opposed to free-form line segments. Both fill and stroke attributes are active when the Pen tool is in use. Lines are created through end or anchor points that can be manipulated to achieve precise design elements. To make an anchor, simply click on the stage to create your start point. Click elsewhere on the stage to create your end point. The line segment is now drawn between these two points. To create curves, click and drag on the stage, and you will see curve handlers that let you modify the arc of the curve. To move any of these anchor points, use the Arrow tool.

> **TIP**
>
> As with the Line tool, hold the Shift key to create any 45-degree angle line you wish.

Depending on how you use the Pen tool, appropriate types of icons appear at the lower-right corner of the Pen icon. The icons and their respective meanings are listed in Table 6.2.

Table 6.2   Pen Icons

ICON	MEANING
+	Adds a point to the line segment in the specified location
-	Removes the desired point
^	Changes a point to a corner point
o	Indicates the point is an end point
x	Displayed when the Pen tool is over the stage

Oval and Rectangle Tools

The Oval and Rectangle tools are used to create oval shapes and rectangular shapes, respectively. By adjusting fill and stroke attributes accordingly, you can create shapes with or without fills and shapes with or without strokes. The Oval tool has no modifiers; however, the Rectangle tool has a modifier that lets you make the corners of a rectangular shape rounded or sharp. You can create perfect circles and squares by holding down the Shift key.

The Rectangle tool has a modifier associated with it. This modifier allows rectangles to have rounded corners. It can be accessed by one of two ways. You can either double-click on the Rectangle tool or select the Round Rectangle Radius icon within the Options section of the toolbar. Once selected, a Rectangle Settings dialog box opens, which allows you to enter a numeric value between 0 and 999 for the corner radius.

Painting Tools

The Brush, Eyedropper, Ink Bottle and Paint Bucket are the painting tools that make up the remaining tools in the toolbar. Table 6.3 outlines the different painting tools and their utilization.

Table 6.3 Tools for Painting

TOOL	UTILIZATION
Brush	To create paintlike lines
Eyedropper	To pick style and color of an object
Ink Bottle	To change the stroke attributes of a line
Paint Bucket	To change the fill attributes of a shape

Brush Tool

The Brush tool draws strokes just as a paintbrush would. This tool allows for various stroke widths that can mimic a calligraphy-type effect. Brush-stroke fills can be gradients, bitmaps, or solid.

The Brush tool has several modifiers associated with it. The Brush Size and Brush Shape modifiers are drop-down menus that let you choose a specific size or shape of Brush tool. The Brush Shape modifier provides several angles of stroke. The Brush Lock Fill option is a toggle that controls how Flash handles bitmap or gradient fills. When activated, all areas that are painted with the Brush tool use the same fill.

Eyedropper Tool

The Eyedropper tool lets you sample the color or style of an existing object. When you hover over a line with the Eyedropper tool, a pencil image appears next to the icon. When you click on a line segment, the Eyedropper tool is automatically converted to the Ink Bottle tool.

When you hover over a fill, a brush icon appears. When you click on a fill object, the Eyedropper tool is automatically converted to the Paint Bucket tool.

Ink Bottle Tool

The Ink Bottle tool is used to change the stroke attributes of any and all line segments within a Flash MX document. This tool comes in handy when you need to change the stroke attributes of multiple lines at one time.

Paint Bucket Tool

The Paint Bucket tool is used to fill closed areas. Once you have a color selected for the fill, simply click anywhere in the enclosed area to be filled. The Paint Bucket tool can also be used to define the light source of gradients in a radial fill, and the direction of a linear gradient.

The Paint Bucket tool has one modifier with the following options:

- **Don't Close Gap.** The gap has no effect on the fill.

- **Close Small Gaps.** Any small gaps are closed.

- **Close Medium Gaps.** Small and midsize gaps are closed.

- **Close Large Gaps.** Small, midsize, and large gaps are closed.

Summary

A majority of the tools in the toolbar are drawing and painting tools. You can use the Transform panel and the Transform tool in the toolbar to alter an item's attributes.

Sample Questions

1. Which of the following is a way to scale an object?

    A. The Transform panel

    B. The Transform panel only

    C. The Align panel

    D. The Properties panel only

2. Which types of tools make up a majority of the toolbar?

    A. Text tools

    B. Transform tools

    C. Drawing tools

    D. Selection tools

    E. Painting tools

3. The Paint Bucket tool lets you do which of the following?

    A. Change the size of an object.

    B. Change the stroke color of an object.

    C. Change the fill color of an object.

    D. Change both the fill and stroke of an object.

PART 3

Effective Motion Design and ActionScripting

CHAPTER 7

Buttons

As we learned in Chapter 3, "Flash Building Blocks," there are three types of symbols: movie clips, graphics, and buttons. You use buttons when you need to introduce interactive material to your Macromedia Flash MX presentation. Buttons and movie clips can have instance names; a graphic cannot. This is important because through instance names we can talk to buttons and movie clips via ActionScript. The major difference between a button and a graphic or movie clip is a button's Timeline. Where a movie clip or graphic symbol's Timeline is in sync with the document's Timeline, the button's Timeline is unique to its attributes.

The Four Button Frames

The button's Timeline consists of four named frames (see Figure 7.1): Up, Over, Down, and Hit. See Table 7.1 for their descriptions.

Figure 7.1

The button's Timeline consists of four named frames.

> **TIP**
>
> The end user can see only the contents of the first three states or frames of a button. Since the Hit frame defines the clickable area of a button, it is not visible to the end user.

Table 7.1   The Four Button Frames

FRAME	DESCRIPTION
Up	Corresponds to the active state of the button—what you see when you first enter a presentation
Over	Corresponds to the rollover state of the button—what you see when you hover or roll over the button
Down	Corresponds to the pressed state of a button; this is the state you see whenever you click on a button.
Hit	Corresponds to the button's hot spot—the clickable part of the button, an area that can be smaller or larger than the button graphics. The Hit frame is the best way to create an invisible button.

Creating Buttons

Buttons are created in a similar manner as movie clips and graphic symbols. The main difference is that you select the button behavior in the Create New Symbol dialog box (see Figure 7.2).

Once you create a button, it immediately appears within the document's Library with an icon of a finger pressing on a rectangle (see Figure 7.3). Whenever a symbol is selected on the stage, a blue box appears around it.

Figure 7.2

When creating a button, be sure to select the button behavior in the Create New Symbol dialog box.

Figure 7.3

The button appears in the Library.

Creating Invisible Buttons

An invisible button has a defined Hit state. In fact, the Hit frame is the only frame used in an invisible button; the Up, Over, and Down frames are ignored. An invisible button is created and used when you need to design a portion of your Flash presentation as a hot spot or an image map. For example, you may have a map of a certain geographic area that has several invisible buttons over certain regions. To create an invisible button, simply create your shape within the Hit frame of its Timeline. Once an invisible button is placed on the stage, it appears as a light blue, transparent object.

Changing a Button's Shape

You change a button's shape attributes just as you would any other symbol. You can use any of the transform capabilities found in the Transform panel or the Properties panel. You can also use the free-transform tool within the toolbar to reshape your button. Understand that when you do this, you are reshaping all four frames in your Flash button. If you wish to reshape certain states of your button, then you need to enter symbol editing mode and select which frames you want to reshape.

A button's shape is defined simply by whatever the largest object is within any of its given states. For example, let's say you have a button that starts off as a square in the Up frame. This square then grows or morphs into a rectangle in the Over state. In this example, the button's shape is determined by the height and width of its largest object, which would be the rectangle in the Over frame.

Using a Button in a Document

Once all four states of a button are defined, you can use the button symbol in the Flash document. To do so, you simply drag a copy of the button from the Library onto the document's stage. Within the Flash authoring environment, only the Up state is seen. Remember, to see the other states in action, you need to select Control, Enable Simple Buttons from the top menu.

Button Actions

Button actions are placed on the instance of a button on the stage, and not on the Timeline. Combining buttons with actions lets you create interactivity. These actions dictate where an end user is directed once a button is activated. You can determine this by using the On Mouse Event action. You can create one button and use different instances of the button with their own set of actions on them.

The On Event Handler

The on event handler lets you attach actions to mouse events. It is used in addition to other actions, such as the goto, getURL, and stop actions. Whenever you choose a complimentary action, Flash detects that you are adding this functionality to a button and automatically attaches the on action before it.

The on event handler has many mouse events associated with it. For a list of these and a summary of each one, see Table 7.2.

Table 7.2 Mouse Events

EVENT	MEANING
Press	Mouse button is pressed within the clickable area of a button.
Release	Mouse button is released after a press within the clickable area of a button.
Release Outside	Mouse button is released outside the clickable area of a button, although the press was within the clickable area. This lets the end user change his or her mind after clicking but before releasing.
Key Press	Lets the end user provoke an action when a specified keyboard key is pressed.
Roll Over	Cursor is over the clickable area of a button.
Roll Out	Cursor moves away from the clickable area of a button after being over it.
Drag Over	Mouse button is pressed down within the clickable area of a button. The cursor is then moved outside the button's clickable area with the button still pressed, and the cursor moves back into the button's clickable area.
Drag Out	Mouse button is pressed within the clickable area of a button. The cursor is then moved outside the button's clickable area with the button still pressed.

→ You can add multiple actions to a mouse event. These and other actions are covered in further detail in Chapter 9, "Introduction to ActionScript."

Enabling, Editing, and Testing Buttons

Button symbols can also be tested within the Flash authoring environment. To test a button, select Control, Enable Simple Buttons in the top menu bar. This lets you see what the Over and Down states will look like and if they work without exporting or testing the entire Flash document. Be sure to deselect this option if you want to continue editing this button. If Enable Simple Buttons is still active, it becomes difficult to select the button on the stage to edit it. To select a button that is enabled, use the arrow tool and draw a selection rectangle around the button.

> **NOTE**
>
> If you embed a movie clip in any of the button's Up, Over, or Down states, you will not be able to see the movie clip when you activate Enable Simple Buttons. In order to see the movie clip in action, you have to export or test the whole movie document.

To edit a button, you can either double-click it while it's on the stage to bring it into symbol editing mode, or you can go to the Library and double-click its icon to bring it into symbol editing mode. Once in symbol editing mode, you can manipulate the button's attributes as you would any other object in your Flash document.

Summary

Buttons can have instance names. This is important because with instance names, we can talk to these buttons through ActionScript. The major difference between a button and a graphic or movie clip is the Timeline. The button has a Timeline that consists of four named frames: Up, Over, Down, and Hit. You can embed movie clips or graphic symbols in a movie's Up, Over, and Down frames. When creating an invisible button, Hit is the only frame you use. Combining buttons with actions lets you create interactivity. Button symbols can be tested in the Flash authoring environment.

Sample Questions

1. Which two of the following symbols can have instance names?

   A. Graphics

   B. Audio

   C. Bitmaps

   D. Movie clips

   E. Buttons

2. What does the Hit frame of a button let you do?

  A. Create an invisible button

  B. Define the rollover state of the button

  C. See its contents

  D. Click and drag the button

3. Which of the following is true about the Timeline of a button?

  A. It's just like the Flash MX document's Timeline.

  B. It's just like a movie clip's Timeline.

  C. It's just like a graphic's Timeline.

  D. Its Timeline is unique.

CHAPTER 8

Motion Design

Animation

Let's face it, animation is a key factor and appeal of Macromedia Flash MX. In Flash you can use animation to move objects throughout a presentation and to change their appearance and attributes—whether it's their shape, color, size, or rotation. Although you can make animation using ActionScript, you create the more conventional forms of animation in Flash: frame by frame, motion tweening, guided motion tweening, and shape tweening. Utilizing keyframes in the Timeline produces all three of these forms of animation.

> **NOTE**
>
> Remember that keyframes are special frames that mark where a layer's contents change. Thus, keyframes are what make animation happen. Keyframes define the start and endpoints of any tween animation, and a series of keyframes creates a frame-by-frame animation.

Animation can be a powerful tool in your Flash presentations because it lets you transform objects and information that appear very sophisticated to the end user. The beauty of it all is that Flash does all the animation for you. Let's look at each form of animation in depth.

Frame-by-Frame Animation

One way to create animation in Flash is frame by frame. This method is achieved by using multiple keyframes one after another in the Timeline (see Figure 8.1). In other words, when creating a frame-by-frame animation, the content of each frame changes as the presentation advances. The main advantage of frame-by-frame animation is that it gives you complete control over the animation. The disadvantage of this method is that it becomes time-consuming to create each frame of animation.

Figure 8.1

Here's how frame-by-frame animation looks in the Timeline.

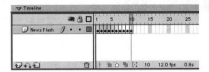

> **NOTE**
>
> The biggest difference between frame-by-frame animation and tweening animation is that with frame-by-frame animation, you manually create the animation with keyframes. With tweening, Flash creates all the sequential animated frames between two keyframes for you.

Motion Tweening

Motion tweening is a great way to create animation without having to create each frame of animation. As compared with frame-by-frame animation, this becomes a major advantage and time-saver. With motion tweening, you simply create the start point and endpoint with keyframes within the Timeline. Then you let Flash do all the in-between frame animation for you (see Figure 8.2).

Figure 8.2

A motion tween has a start point and an endpoint in the Timeline.

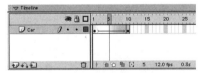

With motion tweening, you can move objects from one place to another within the presentation. You can also scale and rotate objects, as well as modify their opacity. For example, you can use the alpha or brightness attributes to make an object appear to fade in and out. You would leave your first keyframe's symbol untouched and set the last keyframe's symbol attribute of alpha to 0 percent. Once a motion tween is implemented between these two keyframes, Flash creates all the in-between stages of this animation, giving the appearance that the object is fading away.

Only grouped items—such as symbols—can be motion tweened. You must have a symbol in the first and last keyframes because a motion tween can happen only between two symbols. If you attempt to motion tween without symbols in place, Flash creates the motion tween, but also places a new symbol called Tween (#) in your library. This is usually a good visual guide to see if a motion tween has been created incorrectly.

> **NOTE**
>
> Only one symbol on a single layer can be motion tweened. If you want to create multiple motion tweens, you must put each symbol on its own separate layer.

To create a motion tween, first create a start point in your first keyframe. Then create an endpoint in your last keyframe or the point at which you wish the animation to stop. Be certain that both keyframes contain symbols. Also be sure that each keyframe contains only one symbol. Then click any frame between the two keyframes. In the Properties panel, choose Motion from the Tween drop-down list. Your motion tween is created!

> **TIP**
>
> You can also create a motion tween by using either a right-click (Windows) or a Control-click (Macintosh) on any frame in between the two keyframes and selecting Create Motion Tween from the pop-up menu.

Notice all the options for a tween in the Properties panel. The two most important options are Ease and Rotate. The Ease option lets you create the effect of acceleration or deceleration of the animated object. The Rotate option lets the animated object rotate clockwise or counterclockwise. You can also specify the amount of times the object will rotate.

Guided Motion Tweening

A guided motion tween animates an object along a specified path (see Figure 8.3). A good example of when to use this form of animation is if you wanted to create the effect of a ball bouncing onto the stage. To create a guided motion tween, Flash creates a guide layer in which you place your path. Guide layers help you direct objects when creating your document. These layers don't appear in your final small Web format (SWF) file; thus, they don't add to your final SWF file size. You create a motion path within the guide layer, providing a way to create movement along this path from a start point and an end point. The guide layer has an icon of a dotted line in an arched formation next to it.

A single guide layer can affect or guide multiple layers, which must appear below the guide layer. The visual indicator that this guide layer is indeed affecting them is the right indentation in the layers icon and name.

Figure 8.3

A guided motion tween within the Timeline animates an object along a specified path.

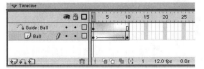

Any layer can become a guide layer. To create a guide layer, select the layer and either click the Add Motion Guide icon or use the pop-up menu and choose the Add Motion Guide option.

> **NOTE**
> Once your path is drawn, make sure that the endpoints of the path snap to the center of both the start-point and endpoint keyframes' objects. If they don't snap to center, your guided motion tween won't work.

Shape Tweening

Like motion tweening, shape tweening can be used for movement, scaling, rotation, and color changes. Unlike motion tweening, however, shape tweening lets you morph objects together from a starting shape to a totally different end shape.

> **NOTE**
> You can also shape tween text. To do so, be sure that you break the text apart so that it becomes an editable object. In order for shape tweens to work, the keyframes involved must contain editable objects.

The other major difference is that, in order for a shape tween to work, the start and endpoints cannot be symbols (see Figure 8.4). In fact, the start and endpoints must be broken apart in order for the shape tween to work. To create a shape tween, create a start point in your first keyframe. Then create an endpoint in your last keyframe or the point at which you wish the animation to stop. Be certain that both keyframes contain editable objects. Then click any frame between the two keyframes. In the Properties panel, select Shape from the Tween drop-down list. Your shape tween is created!

Figure 8.4

Here's a depiction of a shape tween within the Timeline.

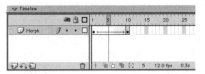

Timeline Notations of Animation

Since all of these animations take place within the Timeline, the Timeline can be an excellent visual tool to see what types of animations are occurring within a document. You can also use the Timeline to troubleshoot any incorrect animations or tweens (see Figure 8.5). All tweens are indicated with a solid arrow between the two keyframes. A shape tween is shown with a green background, and a motion tween is shown with a blue background. A broken or incorrect tween has a broken or dashed arrow.

Figure 8.5

The Timeline displays
notations of assorted
animations.

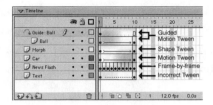

Editing Animation

Editing animation is just as simple as creating it. To edit animation, select a keyframe
and alter its attributes. Flash automatically does the recalculation of the adjusted animation for you.

Importing Graphics and Bitmaps

Since Flash is a vector-based program, you'll need to create intricate artwork, pho-
tography, and collages with additional software. Once created, you can import it
into your Flash document to enhance your presentation. Flash supports a range of
image formats for import, which are outlined in Table 8.1.

Table 8.1   Image Formats Supported by Flash MX

FORMAT	DESCRIPTION
JPEG	Standard file format that is used for Web photos and can be compressed. Use image-editing software to compress before importing.
GIF, BMP	Standard file format that is used for Web graphics and can be compressed. Use image-editing software to compress before importing.
PNG	Importing PNG files from Macromedia Fireworks produces file sizes equal to or smaller than the formats above. PNG files also provide greater editing flexibility because you can import their layers and frames.
Macromedia FreeHand/ Adobe Illustrator (EPS)	These files can be imported to Flash with their layers, frames, and symbols.

Images affect your final file size. When choosing or creating imagery to be used in
Flash, consider the following guidelines:

- Use images only when necessary. Be sure to optimize and compress image
  files as much as possible before importing them into Flash to keep your
  file size as low as possible.

- Always convert images into symbols and use symbols as much as possible throughout your document. Remember that Flash reads a symbol

only once, so your file size doesn't increase when you use the symbol multiple times.

- Scale imagery down to the largest size you'll need within your presentation before importing.

➡ For detailed coverage of the functionality and attributes of symbols, see Chapter 3, "Flash Building Blocks."

Summary

The conventional forms of animation are frame by frame, motion tweening, guided motion tweening, and shape tweening. Frame-by-frame animation is achieved by using multiple keyframes right after each other in the Timeline. With motion tweening, you simply create the start point and endpoint with keyframes in the Timeline, then let Flash do all of the in-between frame animation for you. With shape tweening, you morph objects together from a starting shape to a totally different end shape. The start and endpoints of a shape tween must be editable. Flash supports JPEG, GIF, BMP, PNG, Macromedia FreeHand, and Adobe Illustrator files.

Sample Questions

1. Which of the following must be true in order for a motion tween to occur?

   A. Only the first keyframe needs to be a symbol.

   B. Both the first and last keyframes must contain the same symbol.

   C. Only the last keyframe needs to be a symbol.

   D. Neither keyframe needs to contain symbols.

2. Which of the following must be true in order for a shape tween to occur?

   A. Only the first keyframe needs to be a symbol.

   B. Both keyframes must contain symbols.

   C. Only the last keyframe needs to be a symbol.

   D. Neither keyframe should contain a symbol.

3. Which of the following file formats does Flash MX NOT support?

   A. BMP

   B. JPEG

   C. TXT

   D. PNG

   E. GIF

CHAPTER **9**

Introduction to ActionScript

What Is ActionScript?

ActionScript is Macromedia Flash MX's robust object-oriented scripting language. You may notice that ActionScript syntax closely resembles that of JavaScript. This is because ActionScript is its sister language. With ActionScript, Flash presentations can take on a whole new life by adding interaction and intrigue for the end user. Without ActionScript, Flash would simply play your presentation frame by frame sequentially at the specified frame rate. With the introduction of ActionScript, you have other options. In other words, if you wanted your Flash presentation to stop at a certain point so that an end user could read text or interact with your presentation, you could use ActionScript to tell your Flash document to do so. If you wanted to redirect the end user to another aspect of your presentation once a certain button was pushed, you would do so with ActionScript. If you wanted only a portion of your presentation to loop for a certain duration while other things loaded in the background, you would need ActionScript. ActionScript empowers your end users, letting them maneuver things that they want to see at any given time. Just like its other nuances, Flash makes basic scripting easy by providing a library of scripts to choose from. These scripts can be found in the Actions panel.

Actions Panel

The Actions panel lets you add and edit actions—statements that add interactivity to a movie while it is playing—applied to an object or a frame. It consists primarily of two panes: a library of actions in the left pane, and parameters and the script in the right pane (see Figure 9.1). In the Actions panel's option menu, you can select from two modes: Normal and Export.

NOTE

The left pane of the Actions panel can be collapsed or expanded by clicking the arrow located between the two panes.

Figure 9.1

The Actions panel consist of two main panes.

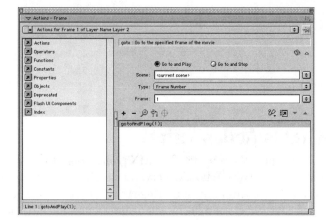

Normal Mode

Normal mode is recommended for those who are just getting introduced to Action-Script. When in Normal mode, the parameters are clearly laid out for you, whether they pertain to an action, a function, an operator, a property, or an object. Figure 9.1 is an example of what the Actions panel looks like in Normal mode.

Expert Mode

Expert mode is appropriate for the more seasoned programmer who feels comfortable enough to write code without the help of the parameters portion of the right pane. Once you're in Expert mode, the parameters section is no longer there (see Figure 9.2). In fact, much of the assistance given to you in Normal mode is gone in Expert mode. But in Expert mode, you're free to write code as you wish.

TIP

When you switch from Expert mode to Normal mode, any code that is not correct is pointed out so you can fix it before you enter Normal mode. This is a handy tool to make sure all of your code is correct.

Figure 9.2

In Expert mode, the
Actions panel leaves
out the parameters
section.

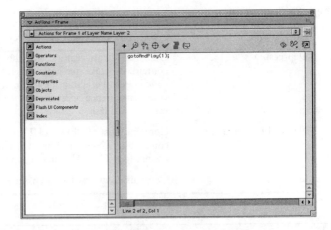

ActionScript Toolbox

A list of all potential ActionScript types is neatly laid out for you in a toolbox in the left pane of the Actions panel (see Figure 9.3). The list is arranged in a branching menu system that lets you pick the appropriate script for any specific need. For example, if you wanted to use an action that controls movie playback, you would select an action from the Movie Clip Control drop-down list. Table 9.1 explains how this ActionScript toolbox is broken down, and when to use each category.

Table 9.1   ActionScript Toolbox Categories

CATEGORIES	CONTENTS AND DEFINITIONS
Actions	Contains a list of all actions that can be added to your script. An action is a statement that adds interactivity to a movie while it is playing.
Operators	Contains a list of all operators that can be used with expressions. (Expressions are any combination of ActionScript symbols that represent a certain value.) An operator is an item that calculates a new value based on one or more values.
Functions	Contains a list of all functions that can be used with expressions. A function is a reusable code block that parameters can be passed to and returns a specific value.
Constants	Contains a list of global constants that can be used with expressions. A constant is an item that does not change.
Properties	Contains a list of all properties that can be used with movie clips. A property is a parameter that defines an object.
Objects	Contains a list of all predefined objects provided by ActionScript. An object is a set of methods and properties.

Table 9.1 (CONTINUED)

CATEGORIES	CONTENTS AND DEFINITIONS
Deprecated	Contains a list of features that should be avoided in new content. A deprecated action is an action that can be coded better with another action. They are kept here for your convenience because they've been in previous versions of Flash.
Flash UI Components	Contains a list of all Flash UI (user interface) components. New to Flash MX, Flash UI components are used for Flash MX–based applications.
Index	Contains an index of all items in alphabetical order.

NOTE

This toolbox of code is available in both Normal and Expert modes.

Figure 9.3

All of Flash MX's ActionScript categories are neatly compiled in a toolbox found in the left pane of the Actions panel.

Adding Action

ScriptActionScript can be applied to an object—a button or movie clip instance—or to a frame. To do so, always be sure you have the item or frame to which you wish to add ActionScript selected first. You can then go through the ActionScript toolbox, find the action you wish to add, and double-click it. Once you select an action, the script is laid out for you in the scripting pane. You can also add ActionScript by clicking the plus sign (+) in the Actions panel. All the items in the ActionScript toolbox are also located in this plus-sign drop-down menu system. Finally, you can write the script out yourself in Expert mode within the scripting pane of the Actions panel. Whenever an action is placed on a frame, it is denoted in the Timeline with a lowercase A (a).

Editing ActionScript

Editing ActionScript is done very similarly to the way you add ActionScript. To edit ActionScript in Normal mode, you can select the line of code that you wish to edit and change its parameters within the parameters portion of the Actions panel. To edit in Expert mode, simply go into the scripting pane of the Actions panel, select the code you wish to edit, and type over it.

To delete ActionScript in Normal mode, select the script in the scripting pane and click the minus sign (–) in the Actions panel, which is located right next to the plus sign (+). In Expert mode, simply select the script to be deleted and press the Delete button on your keyboard.

ActionScript Syntax

Like any other language, ActionScript has rules of grammar and punctuation. How these rules are used will determine the meaning of what's being scripted. Let's take a look at what key attributes make up ActionScript's syntax.

Dot Syntax

In ActionScript, dot syntax is used to put objects, properties, and methods together to form statements. It is also used to indicate the target path to a movie clip, function, object, or variable. A dot syntax expression begins with the name of the item followed by a dot (.) and ends with the element you wish to specify.

Dot syntax uses two main aliases: _root and _parent. The alias _root refers to the Flash document's main Timeline. This alias can be used to create an absolute target path. The alias _parent refers to a movie clip in which another movie clip resides. This alias can be used to create a relative target path.

Keywords

ActionScript has a list of words that are placed on reserve for specific use, so you cannot use them as a variable or function. Below is a list of these keywords:

- break
- case
- continue
- default
- delete
- else
- for
- function
- if
- in

- instanceof
- new
- return
- switch
- this
- typeof
- var
- void
- while
- with

Comments

Comments, which are used to add notes to your ActionScript, come in handy to note what script does what. They also help when you need to pass your document off to another team of people who need to work on your Flash MX document. Comments can be added by using the Actions panel. When you choose the Comment action from the Actions panel, two forward slashes (//) appear in your script, followed by the comment. By default, comments are rendered pink in the Actions panel. Comments don't add file size to your final exported movie.

> **NOTE**
> Comments don't need to follow the rules and syntax of ActionScript. You can type them in any way you wish.

Semicolons

Just as an English statement closes with a period, an exclamation point, or a question mark, an ActionScript statement closes with a semicolon. If a semicolon is not at the end of a statement, Flash still renders your script successfully. Just get in the habit of closing all statements with a semicolon to follow proper ActionScript syntax.

Parentheses

Whenever you are defining or talking to a function, you need to place any and all parameters within parentheses.

Curly Braces

Curly braces are another form of punctuation that ActionScript uses frequently. ActionScript statements are grouped with curly braces ({ }). These curly braces are usually found separated on different lines to make all related ActionScript statements easier to read and follow.

Summary

ActionScript is Flash's object-oriented scripting language. It is the sister language to JavaScript. The Actions panel lets you add and edit actions applied to an object or a frame. You can do so in two modes: Normal and Expert. When in Normal mode, parameters are clearly laid out for you. When in Expert mode, the parameter section is no longer present. All of Flash's ActionScript subcategories are neatly compiled in a toolbox in the left pane of the Actions panel. ActionScript has rules of grammar and punctuation, which make up its syntax.

Sample Questions

1. Which two of the following are attributes of ActionScript syntax?

    A. HTML

    B. Semicolons

    C. Kerning

    D. Java

    E. dot syntax

2. Which of the following must be true about ActionScript?

    A. It is the sister language of C++.

    B. It is the sister language of Java.

    C. It is the sister language of HTML.

    D. It is an object-oriented scripting language.

3. The Actions panel is used to do which one of the following:

   A. Add ActionScript to an instance of a graphic

   B. Add ActionScript to an instance of a button

   C. Edit symbols

   D. Edit graphics

CHAPTER 10

Events

What Is an Event?

Simply put, an event is something that Macromedia Flash MX can recognize and react to. Events are actions that occur while a movie plays. For example, a mouse button is full of events. A button click and rollover are events that take place within that button. All mouse movements are events. With so many Events going on, Flash needs a way to detect and react to them. This is done through Event handlers.

Using Event Handlers

Event handlers perform specific actions in reaction to events. The handler for a Button event is called an On Button event. The handler for a movie clip is an On Clip event. Event handlers are associated with specific Flash objects. For example, button presses and rollovers are all associated with the Button object. Let's take a look at how we would script an event.

Programming Events

To add an event to a button or a movie clip instance, you must first make sure you have the object selected. Then choose the action you wish to perform from the Actions panel. Once you select the action, Flash automatically places the on event handler code as the first line to trigger the action. If you select this first line of code in Normal mode, you can edit the parameters (see Figure 10.1). Next, we're going to look at button events and clip events.

Figure 10.1

In Normal mode, button event parameters can be edited.

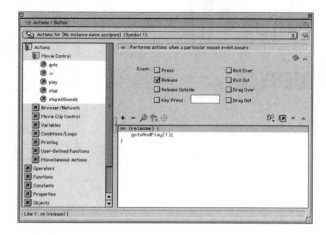

> **NOTE**
>
> If you select an object on the stage that cannot have an event added to it, all of the actions in the Actions panel will appear grayed out. If you're trying to select options in the Actions panel and all of the actions are grayed out, make sure either the object is selected or it is an object that can have actions.

Button Events

The Button event handler dictates what will happen when a certain event is evoked by the end user. Table 10.1 outlines the different Button events and how they are triggered.

Table 10.1 Button Events

BUTTON EVENT	TRIGGER
Press	The cursor is over the hit area and the mouse button is pressed.
Release	The cursor is over the hit area and the mouse button is pressed and released.
Release Outside	The cursor is over the hit area and the mouse button is pressed and then released outside the hit area.
Roll Over	The cursor moves over the hit area.
Roll Out	The cursor moves away from and off the hit area.
Drag Over	The cursor is over the hit area and the mouse button is pressed. Then the cursor is moved off the hit area and back over the hit area while the button remains pressed.

Table 10.1 (CONTINUED)

BUTTON EVENT	TRIGGER
Drag Out	The cursor is over the hit area and the mouse button is pressed. Then the cursor is moved off the hit area while the button remains pressed.
Key Press	A specified key on the keyboard is pressed.

Clip Events

The Clip event handler is very similar to the Button event handler. Clip events dictate what will happen when a certain event is evoked by playback in Flash (see Figure 10.2).

Figure 10.2

Notice all the clip event parameters that can be edited.

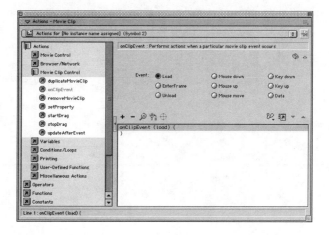

Table 10.2 outlines the various Clip events and how they are triggered.

Table 10.2 Clip Events

CLIP EVENT	TRIGGER
Mouse Down	The mouse button is pressed.
Mouse Up	The mouse button is released.
Mouse Move	The mouse is moved.
Key Down	A key on the keyboard is pressed.
Key Up	A key on the keyboard is released.
Enter Frame	Each frame of the movie clip is updated.
Load	The movie clip first appears in the Timeline.

Table 10.2 (CONTINUED)

CLIP EVENT	TRIGGER
Unload	The first frame after the movie clip is removed from the Timeline.
Data	When either external data or Small Web Format (SWF) movies are loaded into the movie clip with the action `loadVariables` or `loadMovie`.

Summary

Events are actions that occur while a movie plays. Event handlers perform specific actions in reaction to events. There are several specific event handlers for both buttons and movies.

Sample Questions

1. Which two of the following can have an event associated with them?

    A. Button

    B. Static text

    C. Motion Guide Layer

    D. Movie clip

    E. Graphic

2. Which of the following is a Button event?

    A. Mouse down

    B. Mouse up

    C. Load

    D. Press

3. Which of the following is a Clip event?

    A. Mouse down

    B. Press

    C. Release

    D. Roll Out

CHAPTER 11

Variables

What Is a Variable?

Think of a variable as a container that holds information. Variables can be created, changed, discarded, and updated. Whenever you need to capture and store information, a variable is involved. For example, when an end user is filling out a data form, the fields are set up as variables to capture the information. Variables play a key role in any Macromedia Flash MX document that involves interactivity and the capturing of information. In this chapter we will explore the concept of variables, and how they play such a key role in managing information in Flash.

Scope of a Variable

The first time you assign information to a variable is known as "initializing" the variable. To initialize a variable in Normal mode, you use the command set variable. This command adds value to a variable. In Expert mode, you simply type out your statement. When scripting an initialization, be sure that your variable is to the left, followed by an equal sign, and then the value of the variable to the right:

```
mySize=150;
```

Once you've initialized a variable, it belongs in the Timeline you create it in. This is the *scope* of the variable—the location where your variable has some meaning and can now be used. Think of a variable's scope as its location. For example, using the example script above, if you initialize a variable within myMovieClip, then the variable is scoped to that movie clip.

To have access to a variable anytime or anywhere within your Flash movie, you can initialize a global variable. The beauty of a global variable is that it is scoped to all

Timelines throughout your document. You can call a global variable anytime simply by referencing its name. To create a global variable, you precede the variable name with the identifier _global. For example:

```
_global.weightFactor=100
```

Once the weight factor has been identified as a global variable, you can call its contents at any point in the Flash document.

TIP

You can also modify the contents of a global variable. To do so, simply use the _global identifier with the variable name, and then define its new value.

Expressions

In any action or method that requires parameters, you can place a variable or an expression instead of a fixed value. That said, variables can store any type of data. You can use them to hold Boolean values such as true and false statements, and you can use them to assign other variables a value.

Expressions are formulas that combine variables with other variables or values. Therefore, an expression may contain variables, properties, and objects that need to be solved or figured out to determine its value. An expression's value must be calculated before it is assigned to the variable name.

Another way to use variables is as tracking devices. Instead of taking the place of a specific parameter, a tracking variable keeps track of the number of times certain occurrences happen. This information is stored and can be used later. For example, the correct answers to a test can be stored and used to compare against the end user's answers to determine how many people answered correctly.

Data Types

Variables can hold various types of information. These various types of information are known as data types. Data types can be changed very easily, but it is always good practice to keep them constant so that you can keep track of results better and dismiss any unexpected results. Table 11.1 lists and describes the data types a variable can hold.

NOTE

Within a Boolean data type, you can also use a value of 1 for true and a value of 0 for false.

Table 11.1 Data Types

DATA TYPE	DESCRIPTION
Number	A numeric value.
String	A sequence of characters, numbers, or symbols.
Boolean	A value that is either true or false. The words are not enclosed in quotation marks.
Object	The name of an object that you create from a constructor function.
Null	A value that has no data.
Undefined	A value of a variable that has yet to be assigned a value.

Naming Variables

Flash variables must have unique names. You want your variable names to be as descriptive as possible so you can more easily keep track of them and, more specifically, what type of information they hold. Below are three key factors to remember when naming variables:

- The name must be unique within its scope.

- The name must be a valid identifier.

- The name cannot be a Flash keyword, nor a Boolean keyword.

For example, if you have created a form, and one of the text fields requires the end user's email address, a good variable name for this input field would be userEmail.

Loading Variables

One of the key factors and appeals of Flash is that you don't always have to initialize your variables within the Flash document. Flash gives you the power to read variables from external sources as well, such as a text file, a database query, a middleware script (CGI, PHP, JSP, ASP, ColdFusion, and so on), and HTML tags. The ability to read from external sources makes it easier to update your Flash movie because, instead of opening Flash to edit your document and publishing it again, you can simply update the external file. For example, let's say you have content within a Flash document that needs to be updated on a daily basis. You could set that up to read from an external text file. This becomes extremely handy when you create a Web site or application and want to update some information within. You don't need to know Flash in order to update the information; all you need to know is how to use NotePad (Windows) or SimpleText (Macintosh).

TIP

When creating your external text file, write it without any line breaks or spaces and try to use only an ampersand instead of the word 'and.' Flash will understand an external text file better this way.

To load an external file, you must first set it up to be loaded. Be sure that the external file is located in the same directory as your final published movie. Select a keyframe at which point you want this variable to be loaded. In the Actions panel's toolbox, select Actions, Browser/Network, `loadVariablesNum`. In Normal mode, three parameters must be defined (see Figure 11.1).

NOTE

Flash loads the variables from your external file to the root Timeline or level 0. These variables are now scoped to `_root`.

If you would like more control over your externally loaded data, use the `LoadVars` object, as opposed to the `loadVariables` command. The `LoadVars` object has its own properties, methods, and events to handle and manipulate incoming and outgoing data. All that the `LoadVars` object requires is a name and value format.

Figure 11.1

`loadVariablesNum` requires three parameters to be defined.

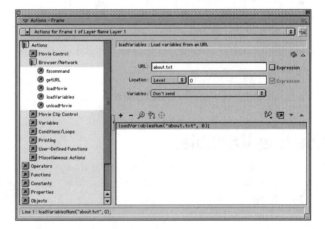

Summary

Variables are containers that hold information. The first time you assign information to a variable, you are initializing the variable. The scope of a variable is the location where your variable has some meaning and can be used. A global variable is scoped to all Timelines throughout your document. Flash variables must have unique names. Flash gives you the power to read variables from external sources.

Sample Questions

1. Which two of the following are true when you're naming a variable?

   A. The name must be typed in all caps.

   B. The variable doesn't need a name.

   C. The name must be a valid identifier.

   D. The name must match the name of a symbol in the Library.

   E. The name must be unique within its scope.

2. Which of the following is a data type of a variable?

   A. Number.

   B. Expression.

   C. Frame.

   D. Method.

3. How can you load external variables?

   A. Through an external text file.

   B. By calling the `LoadVars` object.

   C. By calling the `loadVariables` action.

   D. Through a URL.

   E. All of the above.

CHAPTER 12

Functions

What Is a Function?

Think of functions as the organizers of Macromedia Flash MX. They group related ActionScript statements to perform a specific task. Often you need to write code to perform certain tasks over and over again. Functions eliminate duplication of code because the code can remain in one place, and you can call on it wherever and whenever you wish. Functions are blocks of reusable code that can be passed certain parameters and will return a value. Following is an example of a function that returns the square of parameter z:

```
function sqr(z) {
     Return z * z;
}
```

Flash MX Functions

Flash has built-in functions that let you access certain information. For example, through the use of functions you could ascertain which version of the Macromedia Flash Player end users have on their computers. Functions that belong to an object are called methods.

→ For a more detailed discussion of methods, see Chapter 14, "Methods."

Each function has its own characteristics. Some functions require that you pass certain values. All of the built-in functions are outlined in Table 12.1.

Table 12.1   Built-in Functions

FUNCTION	USAGE
Boolean	Converts the argument to a Boolean data type.
escape	Converts the argument to a string and encodes in URL format.
eval	Accesses objects, movie clips, variables, and properties by name, based on the argument.
getProperty	Returns the value of the argument for the movie clip instance.
getTimer	Returns the number of milliseconds that have elapsed since the movie started playing.
getVersion	Returns a string showing the Flash Player version and some platform information.
isFinite	Tests to see if the argument is finite and returns true if it is.
isNaN	Tests the argument to see if the value is not a number and returns true if it is not.
number	Converts a string to a number data type.
parseFloat	Converts a string to a floating-point number.
parseInt	Converts a string to an integer number.
string	Converts a number to a string data type.
targetPath	Returns a string containing the target path in slash notation.
unescape	Decodes the argument from URL format and returns a string.

NOTE

There are several string functions as well. However, these string functions are now deprecated in Flash MX.

Using Functions

Any function—built-in or custom-written—can be used by calling its name followed by parentheses. All parameters that are sent to a function must be enclosed in parentheses. If there are no parameters being sent, you would simply leave the parentheses blank. Following is an example of a function that takes the parameters userName and score:

```
function scoreTally(userName, score) {
    score.display = userName;
    score.display = score;
}
```

Functions are added via the Actions toolbox in the Actions panel (see Figure 12.1).

Figure 12.1

Functions are added through the toolbox of the Actions panel.

In Normal mode, select the command `evaluate` from the Actions toolbox. Now fill in any parameters in the parameters pane. In Expert mode, enter the function name and any parameters to be passed directly in the script pane of the Actions panel.

Function Literals

A function literal is defined in an expression, as opposed to being a standalone function. The biggest difference between a function literal and a function is that a function literal is not reusable. Following is an example of a function literal:

```
Sqr = function(z) { return this.z * z; };
```

Summary

Functions are the organizers of Flash MX. They group related ActionScript statements to perform a specific task. They are blocks of reusable code that can be passed certain parameters and return a value. Function literals are defined in an expression, as opposed to being a standalone function.

Sample Questions

1. Which two of the following are true about functions?

   A. They organize the toolbox of the Actions panel.

   B. By default, they are rendered in pink within the script pane of the Actions panel.

   C. They tend to be in multiple places within code and look unorganized.

   D. They are blocks of reusable code.

   E. They group related ActionScript statements to perform a specific task.

2. Which of the following is not a Flash MX built-in function?

   A. `Boolean`

   B. `edit`

   C. `eval`

   D. `getTimer`

3. Which of the following is true of function literals?

   A. They are not editable.

   B. They are not reusable.

   C. They are reusable.

   D. They are exactly like functions.

CHAPTER 13

Objects

What Is an Object?

Objects are data types that you create in Macromedia Flash MX and use to control a movie. They are collections of properties and methods. A few examples of an object's data types are sound, graphics, and text (which will be outlined within the Flash MX Objects section). All the objects that you use or create belong to a larger collective known as a "class." Flash provides predefined classes for you to use that are referred to as "objects." An object or class in ActionScript is the equivalent of the noun in a sentence.

Flash MX Objects

Flash has a number of built-in objects that can be found within the Actions panel's toolbox (see Figure 13.1). These objects can help you do a number of things in your Flash document. Below is a partial list of objects that can be found in Flash:

- Array
- Button
- Color
- Date
- Key
- Math
- Mouse

- Movie Clip
- Selection
- Sound
- Stage
- String
- TextField
- TextFormat

Figure 13.1

The Actions panel's toolbox houses the Flash MX predefined objects.

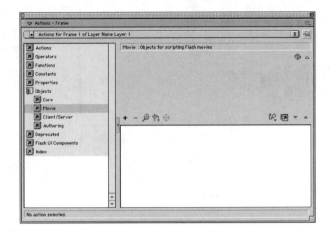

Naming Objects

Before you can use objects you must name or identify them. For example, let's say you have three kinds of fruit in front of you: an apple, an orange, and a banana. All three are objects that can be called by name, and they all belong to a bigger group or class called fruit. They would be named as follows:

```
Friut.apple
Fruit.orange
Fruit.banana
```

> NOTE
> Creating an instance name for an object or a class is very similar to the process of creating an instance name for a symbol.

Once you create an instance name, use the keyword new to create a unique name for the object. You can find this keyword in the Actions panel's toolbox. Any object that requires you to make a new instance of that object will include the new command. You can also create your own objects by using existing objects and properties and calling certain functions.

Summary

Objects are data types that you create in Flash and use to control a movie. Flash also has built-in objects, which can be found in the Actions panel's toolbox; these objects can help you do a number of things within your Flash document. Before you can use objects, you must name or identify them.

Sample Questions

1. Which two of the following are true about objects?

   A. They organize the toolbox of the Actions panel.

   B. By default, they are rendered in pink within the Script pane of the Actions panel.

   C. They tend to be in multiple places in code and look unorganized.

   D. They can belong to a class.

   E. They are data types that you create in Flash and use to control a movie.

2. Which of the following is not a Flash MX built-in object?

   A. Array

   B. Graphic

   C. Date

   D. String

3. Which of the following is true about objects?

   A. They are not editable.

   B. They are collections of properties and methods.

   C. They are another name for Library symbols.

   D. They are exactly like functions.

CHAPTER **14**

Methods

What Is a Method?

A method is a function that an object can do or perform. After the method's function is assigned, it can be referenced as a method of that object. A good analogy for remembering the role of methods in ActionScript is to think of nouns and verbs. Verbs are to nouns as methods are to objects, with the object being the noun and the method being the verb.

Flash MX Methods

Each Flash object or class has its own list of methods that are associated with it. Table 14.1 outlines what methods can be called within the Sound object.

➔ For a list of Flash MX objects, see Chapter 13, "Objects."

Table 14.1   Sound Object

METHOD	DESCRIPTION
new Sound	Creates a new Sound object.
attachSound	Attaches a sound file from the Library to the Sound object.
getBytesLoaded	Returns the number of bytes or data loaded for the Sound object.
getBytesTotal	Returns the total number of bytes or data loaded for the Sound object.
getPan	Returns the pan level assigned.
getTransform	Returns the sound transformation information assigned.

Table 14.1 (CONTINUED)

METHOD	DESCRIPTION
getVolume	Returns the volume level assigned.
loadSound	Loads an MP3 file.
setPan	Sets the left-to-right balance of sound.
setTransform	Sets how the left and right sounds are distributed through the left and right speakers.
setVolume	Sets the percentage of the volume level.
start	Starts the playback of the attached sound.
stop	Stops the playback of the attached sound.

Naming and Calling Methods

After you've created a new object, you can call its methods. You call a method by using the object's instance name, followed by a dot, then the method. In Normal mode, in the Actions panel's toolbox, simply select the method of that specific object to call its method. For example:

```
newDate = currentDate.getMinutes();
```

There are three ways in which the Actions panel displays methods, depending on which method you choose. The method may need to have the object parameters defined (see Figure14.1). In this case, simply type in the object name within the parameters pane.

Figure 14.1

This method needs an object name.

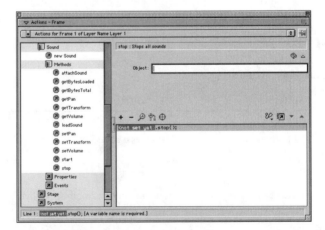

The method may need both an object and parameters specified (see Figure 14.2). You must provide an object name and the required parameters in the Parameters pane.

The method may appear as part of an expression (see Figure 14.3). Here, you must provide the object name before the period.

Figure 14.2

This method needs an object name and parameters defined.

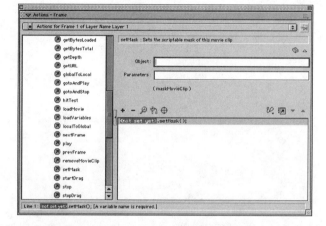

Figure 14.3

This method is part of an expression.

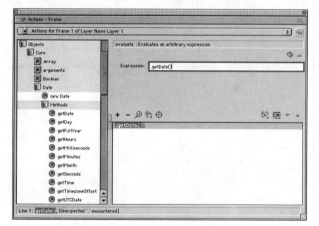

Summary

Methods are functions that an object can do or perform. After a function is assigned, it can be referenced as a method of that object. Each Flash object or class has its own list of methods associated with it. After you have created a new object, you can call its methods. You call a method by using the object's instance name, followed by a dot, then the method.

Sample Questions

1. Which of the following is true about methods?

   A. Methods are assigned to objects.

   B. Methods are assigned to graphics.

   C. Methods are assigned to an EPS external file.

   D. Methods are never assigned.

2. Which of the following is not a method of the Sound object?

   A. `setDate`

   B. `setVolume`

   C. `setPan`

   D. `setTransform`

3. Methods are which of the following?

   A. The same as objects

   B. Functions that an object can perform

   C. Functions that a graphic can perform

   D. The same as classes

PART **4**

Effective Optimization and Output Design

CHAPTER 15

Sound

Sound is another way to heighten an end user's experience. It can add emphasis where you need an end user to focus on something, or it could be a voice-over that describes the services you offer. Adding sound to your Macromedia Flash MX document can bring your presentation to life; however, there are many pros and cons when it comes to using sound in Flash. This chapter outlines those advantages and disadvantages, as well as all the attributes associated with using sound.

Sound Sampling

If you're lucky, you have a keyboard or synthesizer that has every sound effect you could possibly imagine at your fingertips. But the majority of us don't have this luxury, so let's improvise. There are numerous sources out there for you to capture the exact sounds you're looking for. One source is right within Flash, in its Common Library of Sounds. You can access these sounds by selecting Window, Common Libraries, Sounds from the top drop-down menu. Also, several Web sites offer sound clips, loops, and effects available for download. Once you have your arsenal of sounds, you must consider certain factors before making it a part of your Flash document.

Sampling Frequency

Always consider what is the optimal usage for your target audience and published format. If you're working on a CD-ROM–based application, for example, you're not too worried about file compression because a CD-ROM medium can store a lot of information. However, if you're working on a Web site, you want to keep your file size down to minimize download time.

Frequency is how many waves of sound pass a given point in 1 second. This sampling frequency is measured in hertz (Hz) and kilohertz (kHz). The higher the Hz the better the sound. 44.1 kHz is the standard CD publishing rate, while 22 kHz is the standard for Web publishing. Table 15.1 outlines standard sample frequency rates and their related sound quality.

Table 15.1 Sampling Rates and Sound Quality

SAMPLING RATE	QUALITY OF SOUND
48 kHz	Digital audiotape (DAT)
44.1 kHz	CD
22.05 kHz	FM radio
11.025 kHz	High-quality voice

Bit Depth

Bit depth is how many bits of information are being used to store the sound data. Thus, bit depth also determines the quality of sound. Similar to the frequency, the higher the bit depth the better the sound. 16 bit is the standard CD publishing bit rate, while 8 bit is the standard for Web publishing. However, you be the judge. If you find that 16 bit is not adding too much to your published file size, then by all means get the best quality you can. Table 15.2 outlines standard bit depths and their related sound qualities.

Table 15.2 Bit Depth and Sound Quality

BIT DEPTH	QUALITY OF SOUND
16 bit	CD
8 bit	FM radio

File Size

Frequencies and bit rates play roles in your sound file size, but there are other things to consider. Another factor that contributes to file size is the duration of the sound. The longer the sound the bigger the sound file. Also, whether it is stereo or mono will affect the file size. Stereo will double a sound file's size, as opposed to mono. Once again, the value of all these factors will truly depend on the medium you are designing for.

> **TIP**
>
> Always trim your sound files down to as small as possible with sound-editing software. This will ensure that the sound file is at its most efficient for better Flash results, and that it will yield smaller file sizes.

Supported Sound File Formats

Flash can import and export sound files. It supports three main import sound formats: WAV, AIFF, and MP3. Whenever you download sounds from a Web site, you have the option of which file format you would like to download. Whenever you publish or export a Flash document, Flash compresses all files, by default, into an MP3 sound file format.

> **TIP**
>
> As a general rule, always import your sounds uncompressed for the best sound quality you can get. Let Flash do the compressing for you. There's nothing worse than a sound file that's been compressed twice.

Importing Sound

In order to import a sound file into your Flash document, select File, Import from the top drop-down menu, and browse to the sound file. Once you locate the sound that you want to import, select it and click OK. Whenever a sound file is imported, it is automatically stored in the document's Library. In the Library, the sound will appear as a graphic wave image within the Library's top window with a speaker icon next to its name (see Figure 15.1). Also, you can play the sound with the Play and Stop buttons that appear in the top-right corner of the Library window.

Figure 15.1

A sound file is displayed in the Library.

Once a sound has been imported into your document, it can be placed into a Timeline—either the Flash document's Timeline or a movie clip's or button's Timeline. There are two ways to place a sound in the Timeline. One is to select or create a keyframe where you want the sound to be introduced. Once you have the keyframe selected, go to the Library, select the file you wish to insert, and drag it onto the stage.

> **NOTE**
>
> Notice the graphic waveform that appears in the Timeline once you click and drag a sound to the stage. This is a good visual indication that you added the sound correctly, and that the sound is located in the document's Timeline.

Another way to add sound to the Timeline is to select or create the keyframe where you want the sound introduced. Once you do this, the Properties panel becomes populated with sound options (see Figure 15.2). From the sound drop-down list, you can select whichever sound you would like to add to the Timeline.

> **NOTE**
>
> Whenever a sound is imported and stored in the document's Library, those sound files become present and populate the Sound drop-down menu in the Properties panel.

> **TIP**
>
> Whenever you add multiple sounds to the Timeline, make sure you create them on separate layers. Adding a sound to a keyframe that already has sound will overwrite that sound.

Figure 15.2

Sound options populate the Properties panel whenever a frame is selected.

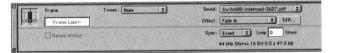

Linking Sound

A sound file doesn't always have to be physically placed on a Timeline. It can also be linked to a Timeline through ActionScript. Select the desired sound in the Library, then right-click (Windows) or Control-click (Macintosh) on it and choose Linkage from the pop-up menu or from the Library's Options pop-up menu. Select Export for ActionScript and Export in First Frame in the Linkage Properties dialog box (see Figure 15.3). Then type in an identifier within the text field and click OK. The sound is now linked to the Timeline and ready to be called.

Figure 15.3

Several options are available in the Linkage Properties dialog box.

Sound Object

As discussed earlier, the sound object has many predefined methods that you can manipulate to utilize sound even more effectively. The sound object comes in handy when you need more control over certain aspects of the sound, such as volume control or turning the sound on and off. Simply put, the sound object is an object that controls the playback of sound.

Summary

Sampling frequency is measured in hertz (Hz) and kilohertz (kHz). The higher the Hz the better the sound. Frequencies and bit rates play roles in your sound file size, as well as the length of the sound and whether it is stereo or mono. Flash MX supports three main import sound formats: WAV, AIFF, and MP3. Once a sound has been imported into your document, it can be placed into a Timeline. A sound file doesn't always have to be placed on a Timeline. It can also be linked to a Timeline through ActionScript. Use the sound object when you need more control over the sound.

Sample Questions

1. Which two of the following play roles in determining the size of a sound file?

   A. Bit rate

   B. Bit rate only

   C. Sampling frequency

   D. Whether it's a WAV or an AIFF

   E. All of the above

2. Which two of the following sound files does Flash MX import?

   A. RealPlayer

   B. PNG

   C. WAV

   D. PSD

   E. AIFF

3. Where is a sound file stored once it's imported into a Flash document?

A. In a button

B. In the document's Library and Timeline

C. In the document's Library

D. In the document's Timeline

CHAPTER 16

File Size Optimization

File optimization is an important aspect of creating powerful, user-friendly Macromedia Flash MX applications and Web sites. You must consider all possible end-user scenarios when creating your Flash document, especially if your final product will be viewed on the Web. Think of your target Web audience: Will your end user be viewing your Flash content on a dial-up modem connection or a high-bandwidth connection? What size monitor will the content be viewed on, and what are the possible screen resolutions? To have a truly successful design, all these questions must be addressed and kept in mind when you create your Flash document. In this chapter, we will look at factors to consider when designing your Flash document to ensure its success and scalability.

Ways to Optimize Your Flash Movie

An architect would never build a house without blueprints, so why would you design a Flash document without some sort of outline or plan of attack? Flash provides several ways to optimize your documents.

First and foremost, if a SWF needs to load large assets, use a preloader. A preloader, simply put, is an entertaining distraction that keeps your end user's attention while the rest of the Flash file loads. The preloader is the first thing the end user sees. For a preloader to work efficiently, its file size must be kept to a minimum. If it takes forever for the preloader to load, you've defeated its purpose. A preloader can be informative or entertaining; it could even be an interactive game. In the meantime, the rest of your Flash content is loading. By the time the preloader has finished playing, your Flash content has been loaded, and your end users can enjoy your entire site without any interruptions or mishaps.

Another way to optimize your Flash movie is to use the `loadMovie` action. This lets you create a number of smaller documents as opposed to one large Flash document. By loading many small movies, you empower your end user to view only the content that they want or need to see. This allows for faster downloads, since they will be downloading only the information that they need to see, as opposed to downloading an entire document.

Another technique is to use those symbols. Remember, Flash reads symbols only once, so one instance of a tree graphic symbol placed on the stage yields the same exported file size as 100 instances of that same tree symbol on the stage. Also, convert everything you use within the stage into a symbol. Symbols take up less space than nonsymbols. Also, make use of shared symbols.

> **NOTE**
>
> Shared symbols let you share a symbol across multiple Flash documents. This not only helps with file size optimization, it also makes life a lot easier when you have to replace the symbol. Simply go into symbol-editing mode of that symbol and make your changes. Whatever changes you implement within that symbol will be reflected throughout all the documents in which it is being used.

What Should Be Kept to a Minimum and Why

Design your document with your target audience in mind. While it may seem cool to you to have a one-minute-long introductory animation of how great you are, ask yourself how many times you've searched high and low for that Skip Intro button when viewing a Flash site on the Web. Does this introduction really serve a purpose? Does it contain crucial information for the end user? If it doesn't, you may want to think twice about including it.

Another thing to ask yourself is how important is that soundtrack that loops over and over and over again in the background of your site? Is it truly adding any value to your content? Remember, sound files can add a tremendous amount of bulk to your published file. There's nothing wrong with using sound because it does heighten the user's experience, but too much sound can become annoying and possibly turn a potential client away. In other words, use sound sparingly.

> **TIP**
>
> If the option of using a mono sound file over a stereo sound file doesn't show too much quality loss, by all means use the mono. Keep in mind that a majority of people connected to the Web do not have their stereos hooked up to their computers and will probably be listening to your audio on inexpensive speaker systems. Therefore, high-quality stereo sound files are wasted.

Similar to the cautions of sound are the cautions of video. Although video can add to the user's experience, use it wisely and sparingly, as it too adds to the size of your Flash movie.

Avoid embedding fonts. Instead, use device fonts in your Flash document. Device fonts are already on the end user's computer. An example of a device font is _sans, which calls fonts such as Arial, Helvetica, or Verdana from a user's system. This saves you from forcing Flash to download font information and thereby increase your file size.

Identifying Optimization Needs

Profiling

You don't have to wait until you've completed your presentation to see how it will look or how it's behaving. Macromedia Flash MX gives you the freedom to profile a document as you create it. This helps you troubleshoot problems as you go—an extremely useful feature, since most of the time Flash documents grow to become quite complex. If we waited until the very end to test our published presentation, it may be difficult to pinpoint where a certain problem is occurring and why. Examining or profiling a Flash document's published presentation is a key component in measuring the success of the final product. Are certain scripts working? Are rollovers within buttons happening the way you envisioned them? Is the presentation too long or too short? Are the sounds crisp? This chapter outlines the key aspects of ensuring success and avoiding surprises when it comes time for final output. Flash gives you various ways to identify where your document needs optimization. The two main tools in retrieving this information are the size reports and the bandwidth profiler.

Previewing Movies

While you're creating your Flash document, you can test the movie anytime to see if all is working properly to that point. This allows you to isolate any problems right away. To test your movie, select Control, Test Movie from the top drop-down menu.

> **TIP**
> The keyboard shortcut to test your movie is Control-Enter (Windows) or Command-Return (Macintosh).

Whenever you test your movie, Flash creates an SWF file of that document for you. When you're previewing your movie, you're brought into the Macromedia Flash Player 6. You can now utilize all the benefits of the standalone player to profile your file. You can also use tools such as the bandwidth profiler and debugging features (see Table 16.1).

When you're in the Flash authoring environment, you can see all the movie clips in action. By previewing a Flash document, you can see if all your movie clips are acting correctly. For example, you can confirm that all the buttons are functioning and animating properly.

> **NOTE**
>
> Although Enable Simple Buttons lets you see your buttons in action while you're in the Flash authoring environment, if you have embedded movie clips in any of the button's frames, you will not see them in action. To see these movie clips, you need to preview the movie.

Table 16.1 Flash Playback Profiling Tools

ASSETS	USAGE
Bandwidth profiler	Shows where certain delays may happen because of large files.
Output window	Pops up when testing a movie to display any errors that may be in your movie, as well as their location.
Debugging feature	Lets you view variables in the movie, set breakpoints, and change values at runtime.
Show streaming	Lets you see the loading of your movie at the current designated debug modem rate. Also used to test the preloader of a movie.

The Bandwidth Profiler

Another tool that helps locate trouble spots in your Flash document is the bandwidth profiler (see Figure 16.1). It lets you see how your movie will act once it downloads. The bandwidth profiler consists of two panes: The left pane displays movie, settings, and state information. In this example, the site is 107 Kbytes' big. To preload the site at a bandwidth or modem connection speed of 4,800 bytes per second, it would take about 15 seconds. all this pertinent information can be retrieved from this left pane.

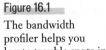

Figure 16.1

The bandwidth profiler helps you locate trouble spots in your Flash document.

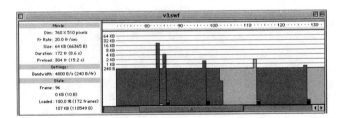

The right pane displays a frame-by-frame bar graph. The numbers along the top indicate frames, and the numbers along the left side indicate the size of these frames. Each bar is measured in kilobytes. In this example, at frame 83 there is something weighing in at about 20 Kbytes. This allows you to check what is occurring at the 83rd frame of this movie. You can then go in and tweak it, thus improving the overall file size of your movie.

To activate the bandwidth profiler, you select View, Bandwidth Profiler from the top drop-down menu in Macromedia Flash Player 6. You are automatically brought into this player whenever you test your movie.

The Output Window

The output window is initiated through the Test Movie control in Flash. If syntax errors are present, this window opens by default, listing any and all errors and their location within the Flash document (see Figure 16.2). If you want to open this window, you simply select Window, Output Window from the top drop-down menu.

Figure 16.2

The output window launches automatically if there are any syntax errors in your Flash document when you run a test movie.

The right pane displays a frame-by-frame bar graph. The numbers along the top indicate frames, and the numbers along the left side indicate the size of these frames. Each bar is measured in kilobytes. In this example, at frame 83 there is something weighing in at about 20 Kbytes. This allows you to check what is occurring at the 83rd frame of this movie. You can then go in and tweak it, thus improving the overall file size of your movie.

To activate the bandwidth profiler, you select View, Bandwidth Profiler from the top drop-down menu in Macromedia Flash Player 6. You are automatically brought into this player whenever you test your movie.

The Debug Feature

Once inside the Macromedia Flash Player 6, you can test your Flash movie on various modem-connection speeds to see how your movie will display at those speeds. These debug features can be found under Debug in the top drop-down menu. Simply select the speed at which you wish to test, and the bandwidth profiler will change and display the suggested results accordingly.

Generating a Size Report

One way to see what items are contributing to the growth of your Flash document's file size is to generate a size report (see Figure 16.3).

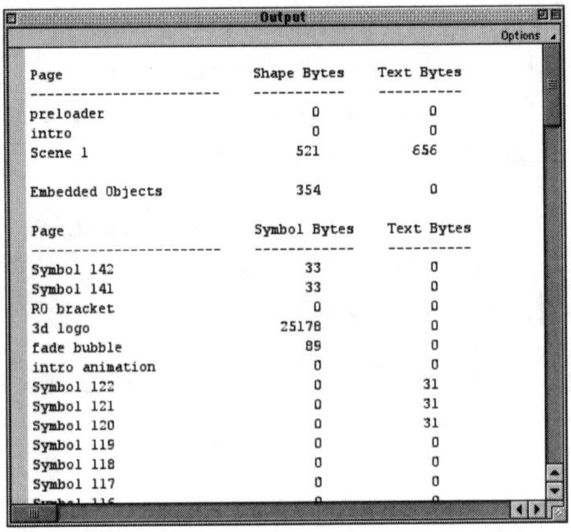

Figure 16.3

Flash can generate a size report to see what items are contributing to your document's file size.

```
                    Output
                                          Options

Page              Shape Bytes   Text Bytes
---------------   -----------   ----------
preloader              0            0
intro                  0            0
Scene 1              521          656

Embedded Objects     354            0

Page              Symbol Bytes  Text Bytes
---------------   ------------  ----------
Symbol 142            33            0
Symbol 141            33            0
RO bracket             0            0
3d logo            25178            0
fade bubble           89            0
intro animation        0            0
Symbol 122             0           31
Symbol 121             0           31
Symbol 120             0           31
Symbol 119             0            0
Symbol 118             0            0
Symbol 117             0            0
```

To generate a size report, select File, Publish Settings from the top drop-down menu. Once you're in the Publish Settings dialog box, be sure to select the Flash check box under Type. Once you do that, a Flash tab becomes available. Click the Flash tab to display all its options (see Figure 16.4). You will see that one of the options is to have Flash generate a size report. Check that option and click the Publish button. Once the SWF file is published, the output window populates with the size report.

This report details every use of all items used in your Flash document, showing each item's file size. Using Figure 16.1, notice the size of the 3-D logo is 25,178 bytes. To bring the size down, you can go into that symbol and tweak some of the information being rendered there, thus improving your overall file size.

Figure 16.4

The Flash format has multiple options to choose from.

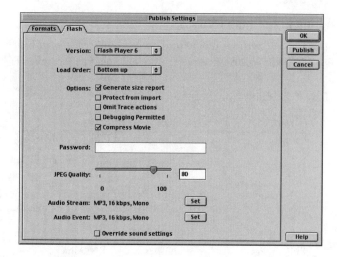

Publish Settings

Flash lets you publish multiple formats at once. To publish your Flash document, select File, Publish Settings from the top drop-down menu. Once you select Publish Settings, the Publish Settings dialog box opens (see Figure 16.5).

Figure 16.5

The Publish Settings dialog box contains all the formats that Flash can publish at once.

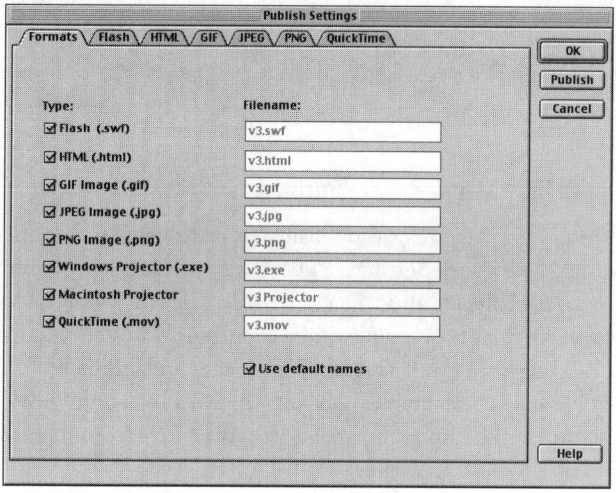

Publishing Flash Movies

The Publish Settings dialog box is where you select your file formats to be published. Table 16.2 outlines all the possible file formats that Flash can publish.

Table 16.2 Publish Settings Formats

FORMAT	FILE PUBLISHED
Flash	Publishes an SWF file, usually to be used on the Web
HTML	Publishes both an SWF and an HTML file to be used on the Web
GIF image	Publishes either a static GIF image or an animated GIF image, depending on your preference
JPEG image	Publishes a static JPEG image
PNG image	Publishes a static PNG image
Windows projector	Publishes an EXE file usually used on CD-ROMs
Macintosh projector	Publishes a Macintosh projector file usually used on CD-ROMs
QuickTime	Publishes a QuickTime MOV file

> **NOTE**
> By default, Flash saves the published files within the same directory as your FLA file. Once you press Publish in the Publish Settings dialog box, all of these file formats are created for you at one time.

Exporting Movies and Images

Whenever a document is published, it is exported to specified formats defined within the Publish Settings. Publish Settings lets you export multiple Flash-supported file formats all at once. In Publish Settings you can specify whether or not a movie, an image, or audio will be exported. Flash lets you export PNG images and JPEG images, as well as static GIF images and animated GIFs. Flash can also export SWF movies, executables, Macintosh projectors, and QuickTime movies. You can also utilize the Export Image and Export Movie commands under the File option in the top drop-down menu.

Editing Publish Formats

As you select file types to be published, the Publish Settings dialog box populates with additional tabs for that particular file formats where applicable. These tabs contain options that can be manipulated depending on your preference for that particular file format (see Figure 16.6).

Figure 16.6

Here are the options that you can specify and edit under the GIF file format.

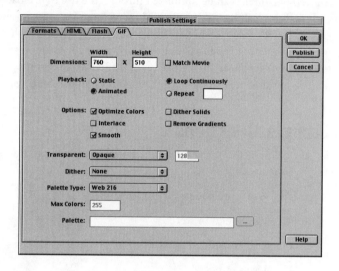

You can also play back movies within the Flash authoring environment. Flash gives you several ways to do this. You can control playback of your movie by using the Controller (see Figure 16.7). To access the Controller, select Window, Controller from the top drop-down menu. The Controller lets you play back the movie in its entirety or move through it frame by frame, forward or backward. You can also jump to the end or the beginning of the presentation.

Figure 16.7

The Controller lets you play back your document within the authoring environment.

> **NOTE**
>
> When conducting playback within the authoring environment, be sure to select Control, Enable Simple Frame Actions to activate actions such as Stop. If you don't do this, the movie will simply play through the document from start to finish.

You can also press the Enter or Return key to allow playback. To stop playback, hit the Enter or Return key again. All these controls can also be found under Control in the top menu.

Summary

A Flash document can be optimized through the use of preloaders, which are several smaller Flash movies as opposed to one big Flash movie, and symbols. Things such as sound, video, embedded fonts, and huge JPEG files should be avoided or used sparingly to keep file sizes low. Flash gives you two tools to retrieve information about your Flash movie: size reports and the bandwidth profiler. Flash lets you publish multiple formats at once through the Publish Settings option.

Sample Questions

1. Which two of the following are effective ways to optimize your Flash document?

   A. Use a preloader.

   B. Use sound in stereo.

   C. Use embedded fonts.

   D. Use symbols.

   E. Don't use symbols.

2. Which of the following file formats can Flash publish?

   A. PSD

   B. PNG

   C. WAV

   D. TIFF

   E. AIFF

3. Which of the following should be kept at a minimum in a Flash document?

   A. Multiple Flash movies

   B. Graphics

   C. Sound

   D. Movie clips

PART **5**

Appendix

Answers

Chapter 1

1. C.   Whichever layer appears at the top of the layer stacking order will be in the foreground.

2. B and E.   The Align panel aligns objects to the stage and to each other, and the Properties panel is used to add frame labels.

3. B.   Assign each frame the label #p to designate what will be printable from Flash Player 6.

Chapter 2

1. C.   You can improve download efficiency by loading crucial information first and trivial animations last.

2. A, D.   Scenes can be duplicated and played back in the order listed in the Scene panel.

3. A.   Flash reads a graphic symbol once, no matter how many times it is used within the movie.

Chapter 3

1. B, D.   Vector-based graphics are drawn mathematically and do not appear pixelated when enlarged.

2. A, B.   The Timeline houses all layers and keyframes.

3. C.   The Timeline houses frames and layers but not symbols. Symbols are located in the Library.

Chapter 4

1. C.   Device fonts do not guarantee the final result is what you designed.

2. A, E.   Static text and input text are types of text formats.

3. D.   Dynamic text fields are used for scrollable text.

Chapter 5

1. D.   `.clr` is considered a swatch file extension.

2. B.   You can export a color palette from the Color Swatches panel.

3. C, E.   The Color Mixer lets you add and create potential swatches.

Chapter 6

1. A.   There are several ways to scale an object. The Transform panel can be used to scale an object.

2. C.   The Drawing tools make up a majority of the toolbar.

3. C.   The Paint bucket tool lets you change the fill color of an object.

Chapter 7

1. D, E.   Both movie clips and buttons are symbols that can have instance names.

2. A.   The Hit frame of a button lets you create an invisible button.

3. D.   The Timeline of a button is unique.

Chapter 8

1. B.   In order for a motion tween to occur, both the first and last keyframes must contain the same symbol.

2. D.   In order for a shape tween to occur, neither keyframe should contain symbols.

3. C.   Flash does not support the TXT file format.

Chapter 9

1. B, E.   Both semicolons and dot syntax are attributes of ActionScript.

2. D.   ActionScript is Flash MX's object-oriented scripting language.

3. B.   The Actions panel is used to add ActionScript to an instance of a button.

Chapter 10

1. A, D.   Both a button and a movie clip can have an event associated with it.

2. D.   Press is a button event.

3. A.   Mouse down is a clip event.

Chapter 11

1. C, E.   When naming a variable, the name must have a valid identifier and be unique within its scope.

2. A.   Number is one of the data types of a variable.

3. E.   You can load external variables through an external text file, by calling the LoadVars object, by calling the loadVariables action, and through a URL.

Chapter 12

1. D, E.   Functions are blocks of reusable code, and they group related ActionScript statements to perform a specific task.

2. B.   Boolean, eval, and getTimer are Flash MX built-in functions; edit is not.

3. B.   Function literals are not reusable.

Chapter 13

1. D, E.   Objects can belong to a class and are data types that you create in Flash to control a movie.

2. B.   A graphic is not an object.

3. B.   Objects are collections of properties and methods.

Chapter 14

1. A.   Methods are assigned to objects.

2. A.   setDate is not a method of the Sound object.

3. B.   Methods are functions that an object can perform.

Chapter 15

1. A, C.   Bit rate and sampling frequency play roles in determining the size of a sound file.

2. C, E.   Flash MX supports WAV and AIFF, as well as MP3.

3. C.   Once a sound file is imported into a Flash document, it is stored within the document's Library.

Chapter 16

1. A, D.   Using a preloader and symbols are effective ways to optimize your Flash document.

2. B.   Flash can publish a PNG image file.

3. C.   The use of sound should be kept to a minimum within a Flash document.

INDEX